Excerpts from
SATAN'S MARK EXPOSED

Throughout the ages tyrants have learned that one of the keys to controlling a population was to dehumanize them. One of the subtle yet most effective ways is to take away a person's name! Chapter 1

* * *

Under the Emergency Banking Regulations ... your bank accounts can be frozen, you could be prohibited from making any withdrawals. The President can activate Emergency powers to control your food supply, control all communication, control all your money and credit. Chapter 2

* * *

From 18 weeks of pumping oil, the Saudis earn enough money to buy General Motors! In 24 weeks, they earn enough to buy Exxon! Chapter 4

* * *

The *"Smart"* Credit Card has a built-in electronic brain. It looks like a normal credit card except that it has a tiny Memory Chip in one corner. That chip ... the size of a dime ... can print out your <u>entire</u> life history **within a few seconds!**

Chapter 6

* * *

The technology is now here to use your television set as a Master Spy system for Antichrist! Chapter 7

* * *

Scientists have discovered that memories can be <u>transferred</u>! And not only that, now memories can be erased! Chapter 10

* * *

Soon a single loaf of bread will cost $8. Three tomatoes will cost $5. And a 10-ounce jar of instant coffee will cost $45. Chapter 12

* * *

First the Government will issue a **Rationing and Zoning Plan.** You will only be allowed to buy a limited amount of food each week. You will also be forced to buy that food in the supermarket in your neighborhood. You will be forbidden to buy anywhere else! A Hand Scan Machine will control your purchases!

Chapter 13

* * *

Christians will be blamed for all the ills of the world! And, because of this, they will suffer persecution. Chapter 16

* * *

All this and much more you will find in the 20 chapters of this exciting and revealing book that provides you with new information that will make **Satan's Mark Exposed!**

DEDICATION

To
MARY ELLEN CASTRO

To
CINDY CALLAHAN

To
CHRISSY HUMPHREYS

Besides my wife, Mary, and our family, there are three faithful friends whose dedication to our ministry is inspiring!

Mary Ellen, Cindy and Chrissy give sacrificially of their time to keep our office running smoothly. Without their generous support I would not be able to write so many books in so short a time. For their tireless efforts, I am extremely grateful!

SATAN'S MARK EXPOSED

by Salem Kirban

Published by SALEM KIRBAN, Inc., Kent Road, Huntingdon Valley, Pennsylvania 19006. Copyright © 1981 by Salem Kirban. Printed in United States of America. All rights reserved, including the right to reproduce this book or portions thereof in any form.

Library of Congress Catalog Card No. 81-80654
ISBN 0-912582-36-7

IMPORTANT!

<u>None</u> of the information presented in this book is intended in any way to undermine any financial institutions or businesses ... <u>nor</u> is it in <u>any way</u> an indictment against them.

Where projection of events are outlined, they are based on what <u>may</u> occur. They are printed as evidence of Bible prophecy being fulfilled in this final hour.

Salem Kirban

CONTENTS

Special Features Include

WHY I WROTE THIS BOOK

We are living in a rapidly changing world! More changes have occurred in the last 20 years than have occurred in the last 2000 years.

The last 20 years have witnessed the most dramatic changes in alignment of nations, in devastating abilities of weapons of war, in growth of superpowers!

Antichrist will not just suddenly emerge as a world figure. The use of the Mark as an identifying system will not suddenly become a reality. **These Tribulation Period events are being nurtured right now in the very era in which we live.** Few people recognize this!

The world is seeking peace. It is looking for a Superman. But peace will never be achieved by man. The tragedy is that many Church leaders are more concerned about building mansions here on earth than reaching the lost with the Gospel of Jesus Christ.

Our political, social, and economic climate is rapidly changing! We are witnessing things occurring today which never would have occurred in the 1940's or 1950's.

Politically, we are seeing the unification of 4 power forces ... the Asiatic bloc, the Russian bloc, the Arab bloc and the European bloc of nations!

Socially, we are witnessing the shocking change of standards in living. Abortion, homosexuality, the reversing of the role of women is bringing us back to the same tragic climate as in the days of Noah. See Luke 17:22-37.

Economically, oil is the lifeblood of the world. The fight for its control could trigger the final war!

Big banks + big oil + big multinational corporations whose allegiance is to big profits are the triangle of power that will strangle freedom.

Politically, socially, economically, the scene is being set for the End Time issuance of a MARKING system. Such a system the world in general will hail as an advancement of mankind. But time will reveal it as Satan's tyranny of terror! That's why it is so important to have **SATAN'S MARK EXPOSED!**

Salem Kirban

Huntingdon Valley, Pennsylvania
U.S.A. June, 1981

1

THE MARK

A Name Makes A Difference!

What greater joy is experienced for a young married couple than the birth of a child. It is a happy time for parents and grandparents alike.

It is at this time that a very important decision is made that will last a lifetime. That baby must have an identification all his own. He or she must be given a name. That name is selected with much thought. And finally an announcement is made.

From then on it is not known as a 6 or 7 pound baby. Suddenly it has developed a personality for it has a **NAME!** The baby may be named George or William or David. If it's a girl it may be a Mary, Helen, Cynthia or Marilyn.

In Ecclesiastes 7:1, we are reminded:

A good name is better than precious ointment

And in Proverbs 22:1:

A good name is rather to be chosen than great riches.

And in Mark 5 we read of the demon-possessed man who ran out from the graveyard just as Jesus was climbing from the boat at Galilee. No one was strong enough to control this man.

Jesus commanded the demon to leave this troubled man. And this is interesting, Jesus asked the demon in Mark 5:9:

What is your name?

And the demon replied:

My name is Legion; for we are many.

Satan's Greatest Triumph

The Arch Enemy Has A Name

Even the arch enemy has a name. His name is Satan. He is also called by at least a dozen other names including: Abaddon (Revelation 9:11), Beelzebub (Matthew 12:24), Belial (2 Corinthians 6:15) and Adversary (1 Peter 5:8).

The demons are those who followed Satan in his original rebellion from Heaven.

Their major purpose is to take away the name of Jesus Christ from the hearts of men and to destroy the individuality of mankind.

It is evident in reading Revelation 13:16-18 that Satan's capstone of triumph will be when the False Prophet in allegiance to Antichrist during the Tribulation Period:

> . . . causes all,
> the small and the great,
> and the rich and the poor,
> and the free men and the slaves,
> to be given a mark on their right hand,
> or on their forehead,
>
> and he provides
> that no one should be able to buy
>   or to sell,
> except the one who has the mark,
> either the name of the beast
>   (Antichrist)
> or the number of his name.
>
> Here is wisdom.
> Let him who has understanding
> calculate the number of the beast,
> for the number is that of a man;
> and his number is
> **666.**

Key to Survival

The key to survival during the Tribulation Period will be an identifying number. You will neither be able to buy or sell without this universal number of loyalty either on your right hand or on your forehead.

First Step to Dehumanization

From Name To Number

Throughout the ages tyrants have learned that one of the keys to controlling a population was to dehumanize them. One of the subtle yet most effective ways to dehumanize a person is to take away a person's name! Even in United States prisons, a person is given a number to replace his name!

Adolph Hitler, during the World War 2 years, placed millions of Jews into concentration camps and tattooed a serial number on their arms. In fact, for those survivors, that tattooed number is still visible!

Up until the 1950's and early 1960's you could make purchases and do your banking based on your name! This is no longer possible! That statement may shock you . . . but it is true!

Just about every transaction you make today is made through a numbering system! Think about that for a moment.

Enter Gradualism

A Sinister Approach

The marking system did not occur overnight. It is one of Satan's subtle strategies to dehumanize mankind in preparation for the Tribulation Period. The theory that is employed is called **GRADUALISM.**

GRADUALISM is that system of achieving social or political changes by almost imperceptible steps or degrees. Imperceptible . . . that's the key . . . so slight and gradual that the mind or senses do not see any real change!

Put a frog in a pot of hot water and he will quickly jump out.

But place him in a pot of cold water and gradually heat it and he will bask in its warmth with a hypnotized tranquility until the water reaches a boiling point and it is too late!

**The
Countdown
Has
Started**

That's exactly the technique Satan is using on us today as we approach the soon coming Rapture. Satan has begun the countdown to gradualism. In fact, if you look back over the last 10 years, you will find Satan has actually accelerated his schedule. If you don't believe me . . . let me ask you a few questions.

When was the last time you boarded an airplane without having to go through a metal detection system?

When was the last time you dialed a phone number using a name exchange such as Central?

When was the last time you mailed a quantity of letters without using a multi-digit zip code?

When was the last time you opened a charge account at any major store without being assigned a number?

When was the last time you made a food purchase in your supermarket without buying an item with a Universal Code system imprinted on it?

When was the last time you ordered a magazine subscription without being assigned a code number?

When was the last time you cashed a check at your bank without writing your account number on the back?

When was the last time you made a major purchase or loan without giving your social security number?

And this is only the tip of the iceberg!

We Are Not A Number

Falling Into The Trap

Several years ago I spoke in a fundamental Baptist school down South. They had so many students that the students had to identify themselves as they came into chapel. I was shocked that they had to give the monitor their identifying NUMBER instead of their name! Even as believers we are falling into the trap of numbering . . . on the excuse that it is more efficient. This is one of the Devil's lies in his steps to dehumanize the world.

It is sad to report that some Christian schools condone a "spy" system where fellow students report on each other for alleged breaking of rules. This often gets out of hand. Friendships are lost because no one knows whom to trust. A fellowship of joy soon becomes one of distrust and fear. The school climate changes. Love becomes overshadowed by legalism. It is this type of "spy" system that will come full circle during the Tribulation Period.

Walk into a delicatessen or bakery and you are told to take a number.

Particularly in the United States . . . we are number happy! And we are playing right into the hands of Satan!

I recall going into a delicatessen one day to buy some lunch meats. They had the standard number dispensing machine. I refused to take a number. The clerk asked for my number and I told him:

When you are ready for me . . .
you can call me by my name.

My name is Salem Kirban.
That's the name my mother gave me.
I am not a number!

He was shocked but he got the message. And he called me by my name.

One of our problems is that we automatically fall into Satan's trap of depersonalization because *"we don't want to cause any waves."* But as Christians it may become our duty . . . yes, our responsibility . . . to avoid any semblance of numbering. Of course, we should do it with graciousness. And we should use this as an opportunity to witness to others of our salvation in Jesus Christ!

2

PRESIDENT'S EMERGENCY POWERS CAN PRODUCE DICTATORSHIP

A Paradox

The President of the United States has limited power and UNLIMITED power!

This statement may seem contradictory to you. On the surface, it is true, but in reality it is not true!

In time of peace, the President's power is severely limited. When people vote in a new President, they think he can bring about sweeping reforms and turn the nation around economically! People soon become disappointed when they realize he cannot fulfill most political promises made on the election trail.

A democracy
cannot exist
as a permanent form of government.

It can exist only
until the voters discover
that they can vote themselves gifts
out of the public treasury.

From that moment on,
the majority always votes
for the candidates
promising the most benefits
from the public treasury . . .
with the result
that democracy always collapses
over a loose fiscal policy,
always to be followed by a
dictatorship.

Alexander Tyler
An early Patriot

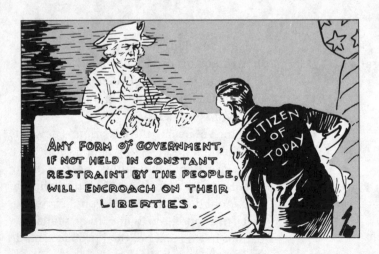

Normally, there are limits to a President's power. In fact, when he arrives at the Oval Office he is surprised just how little power he can wield!

In the real world, presidents have proven less the masters than the temporary captors of a permanent government. The some 3 million government workers have a permanent job . . . the President's usually only lasts 4 years. Thus the power rests in the hands of the permanent part of the government bureaucracy.

Unusual Powers

However, there does come a time when the power of the President is awesome. At a time of crisis, the President has the power to evoke **EMERGENCY POWERS.** Such Emergency Powers give him dictatorial control over the entire population of the United States.

The Senate has realized this. And one co-chairman of a Senate Committee warned that wholesale granting of authority to the president could lead to a dictatorship.

Executives Orders #10995 through 11005 give the President of the United States unlimited power in key control areas.

Executive Orders

Perhaps you did not realize that the U.S. Government can freeze your bank account! The President now has the power to announce the existence of a national emergency via **Executive Order #11921** (June 15, 1976), **#11490** (October 30, 1969) and other Executive Orders. These orders have behind them the force of the law which

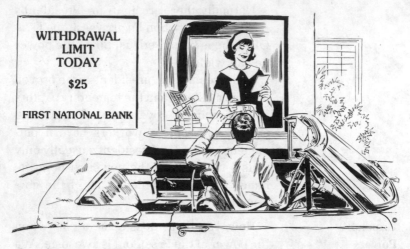

WITHDRAWAL LIMIT TODAY $25

FIRST NATIONAL BANK

One day you will drive up to your bank and discover a limit placed on the amount of money you can withdraw! With financial institutions having only about 5% in liquid cash . . . a run on banks would be disastrous. Withdrawals could be prohibited!

Many people are under the mistaken impression that, *"You have nothing to worry about because your deposits are protected by Government insurance."*

How good is this *"insurance?"*

Bill Baxter of Baxter World Economic Service reports:

> The Federal Savings & Loan Insurance Corporation (FSLIC) insures deposits of its member organizations. It has only a $7 Billion reserve fund backing up total deposits in member institutions of about $600 Billion!

> Most banks advertise Federal Deposit Insurance Corporation (FDIC) insurance totaling up to $100,000 per account. The FDIC has assets of less than $10 Billion covering $888 Billion in deposits! In an emergency, these reserves would be quickly wiped out!

That is why you may one day see this sign as you drive up to your bank's teller window . . . restricting the amount of money you can withdraw!

could be used to establish a federal dictatorship.

Under these orders federal agencies can:

1. Control all food supply
2. Control all money and credit
3. Control all transportation
4. Control all communication
5. Control all public utilities

All this can come into being by the President merely signing a piece of paper stating that a *"national emergency exists."*

EMERGENCY BANKING REGULATIONS

**Towards
One
World**

Under the Emergency Banking Regulation No. 1:

1. Your bank accounts would be immediately frozen, both checking and savings.

2. You could be prohibited from making any withdrawals of cash.

3. You could be prohibited from writing any more checks without the bank's approval, except for *"customary"* amounts. The bank would decide what is *"customary."*

4. No checks would be honored by any bank for any *"unauthorized purpose."*

Such actions, in effect, could allow a President, so inclined, to surrender the sovereignty of the United States and mold it into a one-world, socialistic pattern.

But there's more. Similar laws also allow the President to:

1. Control or prohibit all CB radio transmission;

2. Confiscate "excess and surplus real and personal property" owned by private citizens;

3. Ration virtually the entire output of American industry;

4. Shut down every private school in the country and take possession of the buildings for government use.

There are hundreds of regulations included in this Emergency Powers plan which include seizing property, instituting martial law, controlling travel . . . all which in effect control the lives of American citizens.

POWERFUL CENTRAL GOVERNMENT

Trilateralists Influential

What we are witnessing on a gradual level is the restructuring of the United States into a powerful Federally-controlled nation. Many believe that the Trilateral Commission's immediate wish is more influence over the United States through the Executive Branch. The Trilateral Commission is not merely a passive discussion group but an active influential one. It has been successful in helping to control the Executive Branch of the U.S. Government to move in its desired direction.

Just how close we are to a Presidential Dictatorship in the United States, in the event of an emergency, is anyone's guess.

But in examining the trends of government, the overwhelming complexities of running this runaway monster . . . it is easy to see that we are already in the climate that will nurture a dictatorship.

Yet it will not be forced upon us! This may surprise you. But, as I see it . . . the country will be in such a tragic circumstance economically . . . the people of the nation will welcome any answer to their dilemma! They will clutch at any straw that might offer them salvation from extinction.

This coupled with a threat of war or warlike conditions will make the populace willing pawns in a power struggle for survival.

The pebble of central-controlled power which began in the late 1950's is now a rock. It is rolling out of control and will soon become a boulder that will smash any thing in its way!

Suddenly . . . yet not so suddenly . . . the office of President which once was one of limited power . . . will become one of UNLIMITED POWER!

This will pave the way for the MARK!

And when it does . . only God can save the nation! The price will be a costly one. **It will be fully paid at ARMAGEDDON!**

3

SOCIAL SECURITY ... FROM COMFORT TO CHAOS

No Longer Secure

In 1935 Social Security was enacted as a simple retirement system to be funded by payroll contributions from employees, employers and self-employed persons.

But since then it has grown into a complex bureaucracy that provides everything from pensions to Medicare.

In 1937, an employee's maximum annual Social Security payment was only $30. By 1960, it was $144; by 1970 it jumped to $374.50 and in 1980 to $1,975. It is estimated that by 1990, the figure that employees will be turning over to the government will soar to over $4000!

Presently some $140 Billion in benefits are paid to about 37 Million recipients annually.

There is no security in Social Security and one day Antichrist will manipulate this program to control you! It is very doubtful that you will ever collect even a fraction of the total you have paid in!

Right now Social Security has a DEBT of almost $4 Trillion. Experts say to fulfill these obligations Social Security taxes must ultimately take 20% of the average person's income!

DOLLAR DOOMED

Loss of Purchasing Power

Since 1940, the Dollar has unofficially lost 95% of its purchasing power. It has been doomed since 1940 when inflation began to get a grip on this country.

Take the United States Government Bond as an example. By the time you redeem your bond, inflation has wiped out all of your interest ... and then some! Then to add to your misery ... government officials tax your interest!

Savings accounts in banks give the same end result ... disaster! By the time you adjust for inflation ... you lose money!

WHO CONTROLS GOVERNMENT?

President Limited

Every President tries to cut down on government control but finds little success in doing so! Money continually feeds the bureaucracy that has grown so gigantic it is beyond control!

One out of every six people in the United States now works for the United States government. That is a payroll of over $75 Billion annually!

Presidents are not the masters but, rather, the temporary captors of a permanent government with its own client groups, its own protectors in Congress and its own

THE UNITED STATES GOVERNMENT
Is it getting too BIG?

The BIGGEST Organization on Earth:

EMPLOYS 5.1 million people and pays them 95 BILLION dollars a year!

1 out of every 20 Americans works for the U.S. Government!

OWNS 776 million acres of land or 1/3rd of the Nation

PLUS 470,400 BUILDINGS valued at 126 BILLION dollars!

PLUS about 250 BILLION dollars in EQUIPMENT including 409,000 vehicles, 6,073 airplanes and over 1000 ships.

SPENDS $12 MILLION a MINUTE and this is increasing! That makes almost 13 BILLION DOLLARS A WEEK!

and all this contributes to a **DEBT** of $1 TRILLION DOLLARS with 55 million Americans sharing 1/4 TRILLION dollars of federal income support annually!

settled ways of doing business independently of what its nominal Chief Executive wants.

Presidents come and go at four-year intervals and their appointed administrators last an average 22 months . . . barely long enough to learn the ropes.

THE IRON TRIANGLE

Sub-Governments In Power

Presidents soon make the depressing discovery that they face the **"iron triangle."** The **"iron triangle"** is the permanent alliances of interest among:

1. Government agencies
2. Congressional committees that fund them
3. Constituencies they serve

One government career worker capsules his allegiance as follows:

> I don't care who sits in the Oval Office . . . I depend on Congress for my livelihood!

More than one President has bent his saber trying to buck the system. Franklin Roosevelt called it as futile as trying to push a feather bed. Harry Truman found it as hard as trying to push a wet noodle across a table.

Since then, the octopus government has gotten far more out of control. One official representing former President Carter said:

> There is a series of subgovernments pursuing single interests of one kind or another.

A Budget Out Of Control

**Too Big
To
Fathom!**

The Federal Debt has now exceeded $1 TRILLION Dollars. And this may be hard for you to understand ... but the INTEREST alone on that debt is over $70 BILLION Dollars. That is about 12% of the total U.S. budget! Not that it will help you understand it any more ... but

A Trillion is a THOUSAND BILLIONS

And a Billion is a thousand Millions!

We now have a government whose vast army of regulations is now adding $100 Billion to the cost of goods, while costing the government some $30 Billion to handle the paperwork! To handle this paperwork, almost $1 Million is spent for paper clips and almost $2 Million just for rubber bands!

Look at this amazing statistic!

The United States spends about $400 Billion annually for social services.

> Assuming there are about 60 Million families in the U.S. If the $400 Billion in social services annually were divided and equally given to these 60 Million families ...
>
> Each family would receive some $7000 annually!

But where is most of this money gobbled up? It is absorbed in government bureaucracy and administrative costs!

In 1940 it only took 2½ months of work to pay the annual tax bill. Today, five months of the average worker's pay goes out in federal, state and local taxes.

WHERE DOES IT END?

**A
Bankrupt
Society**

Abraham Ellis, an attorney, who has made an extensive study of the Social Security system, writes in his book, The Social Security Fraud:

> We have already seen
> that there is virtually no cash
> in the so-called Social Security trust
> or reserve fund.
>
> It is full of I.O.U.'s
> with no collateral
> other than the taxing power
> to back them up.
>
> It is hard to conceive
> of a more hopelessly
> bankrupt organization
> than the Social Security System.
>
> It is a simple fact
> that the State has nothing,
> and therefore cannot give to
>   the people
> what it first
> doesn't take from them.[1]

**Enter
A
Dictator!**

What does all this mean? And where do we go from here?

We have tried to show you that the Social Security system that once provided real comfort to those of retirement age is now rapidly heading towards producing chaos!

Part of that chaos is due to the fact that real government control is not in the hands

---

[1] Abraham Ellis, The Social Security Fraud (New York: Arlington House), pp. 194-198.

of the President . . . nor really in the hands of the people! In fact, control is by special interest groups. The day of reckoning has come to these groups because of runaway inflation.

Antichrist In Our Time?

One day someone will come up with what they believe is a brilliant solution . . . a benevolent dictatorship.

We are just about at the point of decision now! It could very well happen in your lifetime.

Many people believe that only by a strong, forceful leader . . . in full command of government . . . can the ills of the nation be solved.

If you are a student of history . . . you will realize that history has a way of repeating itself.

We may be following the same pattern that Germany followed in the 1920's and 1930's.

If we do . . . we can expect the same tragic results. And the troubled Social Security system may be the trigger that swings the United States from comfort to chaos!

4

WHO OWNS AMERICA?

**The
Power
Of
Money**

Lord Halifax said:

*They who are of opinion
that money will do everything
may very well be expected
to do everything for money!*

With money comes power. For the unscrupulous, nothing will stand in their way to achieve the ultimate in power! Such people are driven by greed.

Perhaps the most influential force that will drive us to the climate where the Mark will become an economic necessity is the oil-banking complex!

Big oil and big banks spell big trouble for the world!

It comes as no surprise that two of the ten largest banks in the world (Citicorp and Chase Manhattan Bank) were affiliated with 12 oil companies through a total of 27 directors.

Thus these banks become tightly knit with **OPEC** (Organization of Petroleum-Exporting Countries). Because of this it is only natural that their allegiance is not to the United States but rather to an international community. For if OPEC decided to pull out every last cent deposited in the big U.S. banks . . . it would spell disaster. This is why the major banks held the key to the release of the 52 American hostages. History will prove that the reason their captivity ran 444 days was because of the issue of MONEY!

UNBELIEVABLE WEALTH IN OIL

Shocking Facts

It is difficult for us to understand just how powerful these oil countries are in terms of wealth! In the end, it is money that talks and motivates and controls the actions of nations.

Robert Sherrill, a competent investigative reporter, has pointed out that Saudi Arabia is the nation with the most deposits in the U.S. banks, the most investments in commercial real estate, the most investments in U.S. government securities.

From 18 weeks of pumping oil,
the Saudis earn enough
to buy General Motors!
In 24 weeks they earn enough
to buy Exxon!

The Saudis well know that at any given time they could create a monetary crisis in the United States by selling off their dollars and switching to another currency such as Swiss francs.

HOW DID IT ALL BEGIN

**Soaring
Profits**

THE ENERGY CRISIS...
...a way of life.

How did the United States allow itself to be at the mercy of big oil and big banks?

In 1973 the OPEC nations, with the blessing of the major oil companies, raised their prices some 400%. You can imagine the avalanche of new money that these backward nations received in just one year by this price rise! Their oil income soared from $29 Billion in 1973 to $100 Billion in 1974!

Oil that sold for $2.59 a barrel in 1973 suddenly was selling for $10.95 a barrel in 1974. If you think that was a big increase (and it was) . . . compare $10.95 to what a barrel of oil is selling for today! Or compare what you spend for a gallon of gas or heating oil today to what you spent in 1974!

With such a windfall of billions of dollars in new money, these backward Arab nations didn't know what to do with it. Naturally, U.S. bankers quickly rushed over there and told them what to do with it . . . put it in their banks. Suddenly nationally-minded U.S. banks became internationally-minded!

With this lust for money and their new found pot of gold at the end of their Arab rainbow . . . the big banks urged the U.S. government not to oppose OPEC's staggering price increases.

The World Bank made a confidential study of the situation and, in effect, came up with this analysis of a dangerous trend:

By 1985,
the Arab oil-producing bloc of nations could have $1 TRILLION
to invest
primarily in the United States.

This would be 100 times the value of all the gold
held by the U.S. government!

Concentration Of Wealth

This concentration of wealth in the hands of a few big banks in the United States whose ultimate power is held by Middle East nations spells **CONTROL!**

It is that type of control that could eventually govern who will become President of the United States. It is that type of control that will eventually determine the limits of power. It is that type of control that could strip away any limits of power and make possible a dictatorship. It is that type of control that could pave the way for the **MARK!**

It has been estimated that 90% of OPEC's oil money is handled by only six banks in the United States. Five of these banks are headquartered in New York City.

We got an inkling of what can happen when an oil country decides to withdraw money from the United States. In the fall of 1978, Kuwait (it was rumored) was going to withdraw $2 Billion from U.S. banks. Such a withdrawal would have caused financial panic. The administration quickly bought up $30 Billion worth of dying U.S. dollars on the world market in order to stabilize the shaky predicament! The day was saved. But it turned out that Kuwait had not withdrawn the money. It was only a rumor. But even a rumor touched off a near financial disaster in the U.S.

On November 14, 1979, when Iran announced it was going to pull out its Billions of Dollars from the United States . . . the President acted quickly to declare a national emergency. He froze Iranian assets.

At the end of the Shah's regime . . . almost 8% of Chase Manhattan's total deposits (about $3 billion) was Iranian money!

One can see how big oil controls big banks and how the two, in concert, can control the United States economy and the leaders we elect. No one knows for certain how much OPEC money is deposited in U.S. banks. The estimated figures vary from $40 Billion to $75 Billion. The reason we have no real dollar figure is that oil producers sometimes make their deposits under fictitious names to conceal their identity!

BIRTH OF EUROCURRENCY

A Dangerous Trend

Multinational banks and multinational corporations do not like to be regulated by the United States government or any other government. That is why the big banks threw off their nationalism, with all its Federal Reserve Board restraints, and set up affiliate banks overseas. Here the Federal Reserve Board could not interfere!

Sydney J. Harris

Wanted--a False Messiah

Reprinted by request.

People keep saying "We need a leader" or "We need better leadership," but that is not what they really mean. What most of them are looking for is not a leader, but a Messiah.

They want someone who will give them the Word. And the Word would be one that is agreeable to them, that appeals to their preferences and prejudices, so they can follow it wholeheartedly.

the common good and for the good of their own souls. He is never followed by very many, usually killed by the majority, and venerated only when he is safely dead and need not be taken seriously.

What we are looking for, I am afraid, is neither a true leader nor a true Messiah, but a false Messiah — a man who will give us over-simplified answers, who will justify our ways, who will castigate our enemies, who will vindicate our selfishness as a way of life, and make us comfortable within our

'Chromosome Passports'
For All Forecast by Experts

JERUSALEM, Sept. 16 (Agence France-Presse)—Scientist here forecast this week that before long every person would carry a "chromosome passport" issued at birth by a computerized machine.

Professionally called a karyotype, the passport would contain the genetic analysis of the individual and would be carried like blood-group tags by soldiers and many civilians, the scientists said. Couples contemplating marriage will be expected to exchange karyotypes as well as general health certificates.

This was forecast at the fourth international chromosome conference in Jerusalem, attended by 150 participants from 22 countries.

This gave birth to **"Eurocurrency."** Eurocurrency is an ocean of *"money without a country . . . stateless money."* This includes dollars from the United States (called *"Eurodollars"*) and currencies from other countries. This money floats beyond the reach of national regulators. This is a new phenomena and is a part of the pattern that paves the way for the emergence of ANTICHRIST!

Eurodollars did not come into existence until the mid-1960's. By 1970 there was less than $100 Billion Eurodollars. Today there is over $1 Trillion Eurodollars! And OPEC countries with their surplus billions floating around control much of the Eurodollars as well!

A TIGER BY THE TAIL

Too Much Money

The big oil bankers, who at one time gloated over the billions of dollars floating into their coffers . . . are now having second thoughts!

Continued OPEC price increases bring OPEC additional Billions of Dollars in surplus income. The bankers, once delighted to wallow in this wealth . . . are now afraid they will drown in it!

One chief international economist for a big New York bank estimates that by 1983, OPEC's foreign investments and cash assets will probably reach $500 Billion. What would happen should OPEC countries suddenly decide to withdraw their money from U.S. banks? Especially since right now the

Federal Debt of the United States exceeds $1 TRILLION!

Who would control America?

Big banks simply cannot accept big deposits from OPEC without turning this money around and making a profit. To whom will they loan the money? They have loaned Billions to Third World nations. But Third World nations owe them $150 Billion and cannot pay it back! How can the big banks pay OPEC interest on their money?

Sometime the balloon will burst!

Then who will control America?

The **multinationalists** who are fueled by OPEC's surplus Billions of Dollars!

Who Owns America?

How much longer can we sing, "**My** *country 'tis of thee*"? If we took an accounting right now . . . we may be surprised to learn that we own little of *"my country."* Instead the real owners may be multinational corporations and OPEC!

Understanding this . . . can you understand how the climate is ripe for a world crisis that will force the United States to accept a dictatorship type of government. Or perhaps the United States will be forced to join the European Common Market for its very existence.

In this framework . . . everyone would look for a world leader to rescue them from this dilemma. And he will appear. His name will be **ANTICHRIST.**

He will have a solution! Equal distribution of food and supplies to every person. To insure this equality . . . everyone will have to submit to a MARKING identification system.

This MARK will be on the back of your right hand or on your forehead!

That nightmare is just around the corner!

5

THE BIRTH OF COMPUTERS

The Computer Age

The first computer was born in 1946 at the University of Pennsylvania. It used 18,000 vacuum tubes and occupied a room 30 feet by 50 feet.

Since then computers have made great headway in improvements in design and capability.

While computers do serve worthwhile functions; they will, unfortunately, be used by Satan to dehumanize mankind into subservience to him.

We now have the Supercomputer. The Supercomputers dwarf in abilities the largest business computers made by I.B.M. and other companies.

The new Supercomputers, introduced in 1980, can:

1. *Perform up to 800 Million arithmetic calculations a second.*

2. *Store up to 4 Million words.*

We Will Become Slaves To The Computer

These Supercomputers run from $9 to $17 MILLION each. Quite naturally the biggest customer is the Government. It is estimated that the Federal Government will double the number of computers they now have within the next 5 years!

Microcomputers have tremendous capacities which stagger the mind. As the individual worth decreases in society, computers will exert an ever increasing intelligent control in locations inconceivable today.

Through a Master computer it is now possible to control an entire city using microcomputers as remote *"slave"* computers. Taking directions from the Master computer . . . each terminal would be able to make on-the-spot decisions.

No Where To Hide

To bring this closer to home . . . every store in the country can be tied into every bank or to a central control computer! This means that every purchase . . . regardless how small or in what locality . . . could be controlled by a Master computer at a central headquarters. That central headquarters could have Antichrist as its mastermind.

You Are Quickly Identified

Such technology is already possible and in part, is already being done on a daily basis. Write a check when you buy a dress or book and most likely that store has a check clearing machine. The clerk (or salesperson) pushes keys identifying your bank and your checking account number. Within a split second your check is approved or rejected.

In many large stores, a light wand is passed over the item you purchase. This picks up the identifying number and auto-

There now exists equipment that can positively identify you ... prior to giving you access to a restricted area.

This automatic identification system will employ three verifications of identity:

1. Laser or Visual Identification

A laser beam camera reads the identification number on your forehead and, via computer relay, matches that number with your facial characteristics.

2. Voice Print Identification

A microphone will pick up your voice and match your voice print with the voice print pattern in your computer file.

3. Hand Scan Identification

A laser scanning device will relay your palm print pattern to central computer for rapid identification.

Within a few seconds ... all this data will be analyzed by a Master Computer, cross-matched and verified. If positive, the **ENTER** light will flash on and you may then enter.

Such a machine could be placed at every Supermarket, every Bank. There would be no way to fool it. This Triple Identification System could be programmed to deny entrance to believers and anyone not having the Mark. The technology for this equipment **already** exists. And a prototype appeared in computer magazines as long ago as 1972!

matically tallies it on the cash register and, at the same time, through to central control!

These point-of-sale (POS) terminals are part of the strategy to reduce everything to numbers. Eventually they will contribute to the dehumanization of man. For this same light wand can be passed over your hand or forehead to pick up your identifying number . . . or read your fingerprint!

Micro Computers

We are living in the age of microcomputers. A single chip microprocessor containing over 10,000 transistors is less than the size of a dime! It staggers the imagination to realize what a large volume of information can be stored in so small a unit. Think of the power a world leader will have who can control this mechanical army!

In less than 40 years the computer has come from a dream to a design for disaster!

6

ELECTRONIC BANKING
FIRST STEP TOWARDS
THE MARK

Super
Banks
Emerge

The banks began a revolution in the mid-1960's when they moved into the credit card business. By 1969 ... two major systems emerged ... BankAmericard and Master Charge.

A survey taken in 1975 indicated that over 60% of the then 55-million holders of national bank cards did **not** know which bank issued their cards. They failed to realize that their credit was controlled by **super banks**. At that time major credit cards gave the banks an added $22 billion in sales volume! Small banks could not compete with this service. Thus the larger banks got larger.

**Global
Oriented**

These larger banks are **global oriented** not nationally oriented. Their allegiance is to an international world system . . . for that's where their volume of profits originates. It has been estimated that half of the money loaned by the New York super banks is loaned to worldwide international corporations!

With this international allegiance, it is natural for the super banks to try and build up the use of credit cards in the U.S. This gives them more money to negotiate deals internationally.

In 1975 there were some 55-million credit card holders in the United States. Today there are over 600 million credit cards in use. This generates a sales volume annually of over $150 BILLION. Of this unpaid balances account for over $50 BILLION. It is the interest that banks charge on this $50 BILLION that enlarges their own treasury of power!

Trilateralists Take Control

This so-called plastic revolution could be more aptly called a super bank revolution. It helps fulfill the aims of the Trilateralists who are striving for an international superpower.

Bankers for years now have been wanting to flood the country with a system called **EFT** (Electronic Funds Transfer). It is their primary drive towards a *"cashless society."* They are making great headway right now . . . after a few years of slow progress.

YOUR NAME IS SURE TO BE IN ONE OF THESE COMPUTERS!

The United States Government knows you by a number. And federal agencies are turning to computers ... which, at the touch of a button ... can produce instant information on millions of Americans. Here are some major examples:

SOCIAL SECURITY ADMINISTRATION
Your Social Security number will soon become a universal number.

INTERNAL REVENUE SERVICE
Computer tapes store details from tax returns of over 75 million citizens. These tapes are made available to the 50 States.

U.S. SECRET SERVICE
About 50,000 persons are on computer who might tend to harm or embarrass the President or other high Government officials.

F.B.I.
Fingerprint files of over 86 million people now on computer.

DEPARTMENT OF AGRICULTURE
Keeps data on over 850,000 people.

DEPARTMENT OF TRANSPORTATION
Almost 2.7 million citizens who have been denied driver's licenses are on computer.

PENTAGON
Maintains files on some 7 million military personnel and civilians who have been subjected to *"security, loyalty, criminal and other type investigations."*

VETERANS ADMINISTRATION
Keeps files on 13.5 million veterans and dependents.

DEPARTMENT OF LABOR
Has on computer files on 2 million persons in federally financed work ... all coded by their social security number.

DEPARTMENT OF JUSTICE
Computer bank has names of more than 14,000 individuals who have been involved in riots and civil disorders since mid-1968.

DEPARTMENT OF HOUSING AND URBAN DEVLOPMENT
Maintains records on 4.5 million who have bought F.H.A. homes.

With this federal computer network, there is virtually no limit to the volume of information that can be made available at a moment's notice on just about every American.

The United States government is one of their best customers. Social security money can now be transferred direct to your bank ... without your seeing any check. It is done electronically via computer! This **EFT** system is promoted to the unwary consumer as a *"convenience."* **Actually, it paves the way for Antichrist and the MARK!**

Towards A "Cashless Society"

Debit Cards

In the widely envisioned *"cashless society,"* dominated by magnetically encoded plastic debit cards, funds would be rocketed across the nation in seconds, eliminating checks and supposedly saving both the time and the money it takes to process them. Such a transfer was made electronically to a bank in London in the January, 1981 release of the 52 American hostages from Iran.

With electronic terminals in every retail outlet ... and even in homes and offices, there would be no need for people ever to go near a bank to carry out routine transactions. The plastic credit card would be used for all purchases, deposits, withdrawals, payment of bills and borrowing of money.

In recent years we have seen the spawning of automated teller machines **(ATMs).** This saves banks salaries and increases their profits. They also contain a hidden motion picture camera that photographs and identifies you without your knowledge.

LASER IDENTIFICATION BEAM

One day in the Tribulation Period you will need proper identification to withdraw or deposit money in your bank. That identification will be an invisible mark either on the back of your right hand or on your forehead!

Each teller position will have a Laser Identification Beam that will be used to make your mark visible. You will need this even to cash your Social Security check!

Quite possibly, you may even have to supply your Worldwide Money Card. Remember, a tiny computer chip on your Money Card can contain over 10,000 transistors and store your complete life history and credit record! Can you imagine the power that international bankers and Antichrist will have over the individual with this data at their instant control!

Electronic Funds Transfer (EFT) would cut bank costs about 80% in paper handling. Banks today process some 55 Billion checks annually via the EFT system at a cost of $16 Billion.

> Experts who have studied the awesome growth of EFT believe that someday the nation's approximately 14,000 banks will compress into fewer than 100 national institutions. In the past 15 years it has been estimated that, because of banking monopolies, there have been some 15,000 mergers of businesses. Such mergers give ultimate power to superbanks!

Visa (BankAmericard) and Master Charge as well as American Express Company are rapidly persuading retailers to accept their cards in addition to the retailer's own card. This is becoming highly successful.

Most experts agree that eventually there will be a blending of the two major credit card systems . . . Visa and Master Charge. Actually, for banks that already issue both cards . . . such a merger has already taken place.

The Super Card

Eventually there will be the emergence of just one supercard. A Citibank official commented in the April 18, 1977 issue of Business Week:

> **If there's just one card . . .**
> **it will be issued by the government!**

You and I know that when that occurs . . . we will be in the age of Antichrist!

Electronic banking will control your finances. Eventually everyone will have to have a Mark placed on their right hand or forehead. As you enter a bank, you will place your hand palm down at the teller cage. A beam of light . . . a laser beam . . . will automatically read your Mark number on your hand (or forehead). You will be immediately identified. Your request for money will be instantly approved . . . or denied!

For those living in that era, it will seem like a dream. But, in reality, it will be a **NIGHTMARE!**

"SMART" CREDIT CARDS TO REPLACE CURRENT ONES

The Card With A Brain

The technique of gradualism has been used in the credit card business. First came the ordinary credit card that you and I are familiar with. This revolution began in the mid-60's.

Then came **EFT** (Electronic Funds Transfer). Transaction or Debit cards (also known as asset cards) were issued. This is a plastic credit card issued by a financial institution to account-holding customers. Information is either embossed or impregnated or magnetically encoded so that the card can activate the EFT system. Transactions can be completed in seconds . . . electronically . . . without the necessity of checks, passbooks, deposit slips, etc.

Now we are witnessing the entrance of

the *"Smart"* credit card. It is estimated by computer companies that this *"Smart"* credit card will replace the present-day credit cards and personal checkbooks by early 1990!

**Controlled
By
A
Card**

The *"Smart"* credit card has a built-in electronic brain. It looks like your normal credit card except that it has a tiny memory-chip in one corner. **And that's the difference!**

You first slip this *"Smart"* credit card into a machine that verifies your identity to prove the card was not stolen nor being used improperly. Once your card clears this hurdle . . . you can put it to use.

When making a purchase, a customer inserts the card into the store's electronic *"monster."* This automatically deducts your purchase from its credit load. It records the details of the payment and your bank account on a magnetic band, which acts as the shopkeeper's cash register. Later, the shopkeeper takes this magnetic band to the bank. The bank runs it through their computer, crediting his account and debiting (or charging) your bank account. If the shopkeeper has a terminal in his store . . . this electronic funds transfer takes place at the time you actually make your purchase!

Currently these *"Smart"* credit cards with electronic memory-chips cost some $50 to produce. Soon this cost will be pared down to $5 per card as banks prepare a major drive next year to give them away . . . promoting them as an *"electronic miracle!"*

7

TODAY'S MARKING SYSTEM, TOMORROW'S CONTROL

The System Is Here!

One might ask the question, how could intelligent people allow themselves to be deluded into accepting a Mark so they could buy or sell?

The answer is simple. We are **already** accepting systems of identification control. The Social Security number, initiated in the 1930's as a means only of identifying an individual to see that he received his payments, has almost become a universal identification number in the United States. It is requested when you apply for a job, when you apply for a loan, when you apply for a license plate, etc.

In 1975 the U.S. Passport office suggested everyone in the U.S. be given a unified identification number. The advent of credit cards has also advanced the numbering idea. Soon cash will be outdated. Even checks will be largely phased out of existence in a few years. All or most transactions will be through a plastic credit card that has a number. That number, when passed through a computer, will determine whether or not you can buy merchandise or food.

Now, what food companies have hailed as the greatest invention since the light bulb, has been the creation of a series of vertical stripes on all supermarket items.

This new Universal Product Code is known to most consumers merely as a composite symbol of black bars and numbers appearing on many packages.

When drawn across a scanner at the supermarket checkout station, the symbol identifies the item to a computer, which instantaneously tells the cash register what price to ring up for that product. Within 10 years every supermarket in the United States will have this computer system in operation, controlling the identification of over 200 billion cans, packages and bottles, annually!

Your Hand Is An Identifier!

A Machine Identifies You By Your Hand

But that's not all. An Ohio company, in early 1975, was issued a patent that has an identification apparatus which relies on the characteristic vibrations of the human body.

Acoustical [sound] wave energy can be transmitted from one finger to another and be recorded for later reference!

As an example, this procedure can identify a person who stands on a doormat and places one hand on a doorknob. If the frequency response passing through the body matches the one recorded in the memory device, the applicant is admitted. The characteristics of several thousand individuals can be stored in **one** memory device!

The inventor says this system will be used to provide access to computers and verify credit cards and bank checks.

Special credit cards have also been designed that are used instead of keys to unlock doors!

DON'T BELIEVE RUMORS!

In times of uncertainty, rumors have a way of spreading far faster than fact! It is unfortunate that some rumors appear in print as though they were fact. This gives added speed to the false information and causes both confusion and hysteria.

One rumor ... **without any foundation** ... has been making the rounds regarding Social Security and other monthly benefit checks. The rumor alleged that the Department of the Treasury was issuing monthly benefit checks printed with instructions that, before the check could be cashed, an identifying mark on the wrist or forehead must match an identifying number on the check.

This is not true! It is false!

The Department of the Treasury has advised us that Government checks are preprinted by the manufacturer with the Treasury Seal, dateline and check serial and check symbol numbers on the face of the check. The reverse is also preprinted with the normal encashment instructions, plus a message encouraging people to buy U.S. Savings Bonds.

Over 99% of Treasury issued checks (which include Social Security and IRS tax refund payments) are inscribed as to payee name, payment amount and payment identification numbers by the computer printers. These printers do not have the capability of printing additional messages on the reverse of the checks.

No one yet has produced a physical check with the legend stating that a Mark is required. Such a rumor is without any foundation. To spread such a rumor does a disservice to believers as well as responsible Government officials.

What does this all mean? And how does it affect the Jew? One must keep in mind that in this last 3½ year Tribulation Period not only Jews, but also all Gentiles who turn to Christ (the Tribulation Saints) will be persecuted.

And these sophisticated computer systems, which are already in use . . . to select those eligible to buy food, to be admitted into a house . . . will be used to identify those with the approved Mark!

It is conceivable that the population explosion will be so acute that housing facilities, as well as food, will be in short supply. Naturally those who are loyal to Antichrist, who wear his emblem or Mark, will be those thought worthy to receive priority to buy food and seek housing.

Without the Mark, it may be impossible for you to enter your own home! Your finger vibrations may not be in the memory bank of the lock on your house nor in that of the supermarket where you shop.

Now can you see how events of today make entirely possible Antichrist's actions of tomorrow?

The Enforcer

**Panic
And
Pressure**

How will the False Prophet enforce his edict? One can imagine the pandemonium that breaks out when this announcement is first made to the public. People will rush to the grocery stores to stock up on food perhaps only to find the stores bolted shut

until the marking system has been completed.

In November, 1974 when I was in Israel,
the Israeli pound was devalued some 60%.
People panicked. They flocked into appliance stores trying to buy refrigerators. They
crowded into their grocery stores hoarding
up on food. When the appliance dealer told
them he was sold out of refrigerators they
asked: *"What else do you have, I'll buy
anything!"* Such was the mass hysteria of
the first few days. Some stores closed,
hiding their goods, knowing that with the
raise in prices they would soon realize a
bigger profit.

Naturally, the False Prophet will need a
company of loyal soldiers to enforce his
edict. And no doubt, he will have a spy
system that would make the Gestapo, the
Russian K.G.B. and the United States C.I.A.
turn green with envy.

Such an effective spy system would be
necessary for the enforcement of a loyal
world government.

Towards An International Order

**One
World**

In an expanded edition of his book **American Foreign Policy** published by North in
1974, Henry Kissinger states:

> *We must construct an international
> order before a crisis imposes it as
> a necessity.*

In a speech given in Los Angeles on January 24, 1975 he said that the last quarter of this century

> ... could be remembered as that period when mankind fashioned the first truly global community.

Dr. Kissinger further stated:

> There can be no peaceful international order without a constructive relationship between the United States and the Soviet Union ...

Would such a constructive relationship include the working together of the K.G.B. and the C.I.A.? In light of Bible prophecy, this could be a future possibility.

It was Felix Dzerzhinsky, Russia's first secret police chief, who said:

> We stand for organized terror.

By Any Means

Nor is the C.I.A. above reproach, or the leaders of Government. The C.I.A. has admitted that at times it has operated outside of the scope of their authorization, illegally. The Watergate scandal during the Nixon administration should certainly make people aware of the intrigue, the lies and the power struggle that attempted to thwart the freedom of Americans.

Alexander Solzhenitsyn in his book, *The Gulag Archipelago* (New York, Harper and Row, 1973) told how the K.G.B. extract *"confessions."* Beginning with night arrests, they employ every manner of humiliation to break their victims, including thirst, filth, drugs, deprivation of sleep, threatening loved ones, insect-infested boxes, starvation, the gradual crushing of genitals, scraping the skin off a man's back with a grater till it bled and then oiling it with turpentine!

The 444 day ordeal of the 52 U.S. hostages in Iran give us further insight on what is to come! And it will happen here in America!

The Choice: To Bow Or To Starve

A Tragic Choice

Imagine if you were living in the Tribulation Period. You had a choice: to accept the Mark and be able to buy food and life . . . or to reject the Mark and face persecution and hunger. Slowly you watch as your baby cries in anguish from starvation. Perhaps you witness your husband torn away from you. Held down by soldiers, he is injected with heroin day after day until he is totally relying on the drug. Then, a walking automaton, he is released back to you! How long could you stand it? Would you finally break and accept the Mark? Or would it take some more coaxing like watching your 5-year-old child slowly die by starvation? Would this be the breaking point?

How strong would be your faith? That is just the beginning of what both Jew and Christ-believing Gentile Tribulation Saints may face in the torturous last 3½ years of the Tribulation Period.

When something like this is brought to our attention, we tend to disbelieve it, saying that it will never occur. Yet we fail to realize that such brutality is occurring even today!

Even the world-famous Canadian Royal Mounted Police have used a 39-page manual of instruction as their basis for breaking down an individual. The manual advocates the use of brainwashing, sexism, lies, deceit and deprivation as an *"assault on his dignity."*[1]

Restricted Freedoms

Imagine the day when you cannot automatically go to the supermarket to buy food ... when your freedoms will be so restricted that you and your loved ones may die of starvation, and most won't care.

But, of course, this is not new either. Right now throughout the world thousands of children die of starvation every day but you and I are indifferent to their plight. Why? Perhaps, because we are so busy just trying to keep ourselves alive! This indifference will be amplified during the Tribulation Period.

Imagine the scoffs of the crowd:

> *So they're starving ... it's their own fault. If they would accept the Mark, they would live and have the food they need. Instead, it's their choice for them to follow their God. See if their God will send them manna from Heaven. If He did it once ... let Him do it again!*

Loaded with their bag of groceries, the people will not pity those who refuse to accept the Mark.

---

[1] Philadelphia Inquirer, *UPI, Philadelphia: March 27, 1975, p. 3-A.*

Your Television Set Can Become A SPY NETWORK For ANTICHRIST!

Very shortly . . . you will not be safe . . . EVEN IN YOUR OWN HOME! There is a big push to install cable TV in every home in America!

There are several reasons:

1. MONEY
   Cable TV is big business. One cable TV company stands to make 100 MILLION in just 15 years! Millions of dollars are at stake. It is a lucrative new business.

2. A LAUNDERING OPPORTUNITY
   Opportunities to make money attract underworld characters. Cable TV projects initially can cost $10 to $60 Million to start. Crime syndicates who have made millions on gambling, prostitution, etc. need to "*launder*" or channel this dirty money through a clean business. Cable TV offers this opportunity!

Cable TV has its advantages. You receive a clear picture all the time. There is no outside interference since a cable is run from an outside power line directly into your home and connected to your Television set! The largest cable-television franchise yet awarded will provide cable TV for 400,000 homes in Dallas, Texas. This system in Dallas will take 5 years to complete. It will cost an estimated $100 Million initially. *And here is the next advantage of cable TV* . . . it will offer subscribers up to 80 different channels to select from daily!

What are the far-reaching possible consequences? Right now . . . 1 out of 5 homes with TV sets have cable television. The cable running into your home is connected to your TV. This electronic system can provide an excellent way for the soon-coming ANTICHRIST to intrude on your privacy!

It is expected that very shortly *(if not already)* the technology will exist to convert your TV into a SOUND Camera. Quite possibly, in the near future, Government intelligence will be able to tap into your cable line. By pushing a series of buttons in their headquarters . . . they will be able to look right into your home by way of the TV tube! They will also be able to single out Christians for persecution!

Thus . . . cable TV could become a part of a U.S. spy network to control the population. Christian political action groups will cause a backlash that will trigger an era of intense persecution against anyone who names the name of Christ.

Antichrist . . . a world leader . . . will stop at no means to control those who pose a threat to his successes! We already have highly sophisticated spying devices. *After all, if it is now possible to make a CHIP the size of your thumbnail . . . that can make a Computer TALK . . . does it seem anymore sensational to transform your TV into a SPYING device for a Government leader?*

One Pennsylvania township as recently as October, 1980, was already considering using Cable TV networks to enable police to electronically check what they termed *"trouble-spots."* The most frightening aspect of this entire plan . . . is that this SPY PROGRAM can be carried on through your TV set . . . *without you being aware of it!* While you are watching a TV program . . . <u>BIG BROTHER</u> will be watching and listening to you!

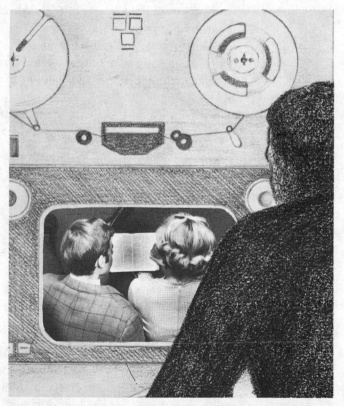

By way of electronics, Antichrist will be able to invade the privacy of your home as you have devotions! In the Tribulation Period Christians will suffer persecution and have nowhere to hide!

8

THE ENTRANCE OF ANTICHRIST

Antichrist Alive!

Antichrist is alive today! That's what I sincerely believe! I could be wrong . . . but I believe he is waiting in the wings . . . just waiting for all the pieces of the puzzle to fit together.

Then he will make his grand entrance. We have already seen how the groundwork is now established for the issuing of the **MARK!**

With the Social Security system out of control the following scenario could occur:

Many people would demand a strong leadership with full authoritative powers.

They will demand that the 3 Million federal work force be drastically reduced and more power given to the President.

The President will issue a decree making it mandatory that everyone be given an identification number so that the wealth of the nation can be spread evenly and fairly.

Under such a leadership, the Social Security number will become your identification number. It will be prefixed by **666** and quite possibly followed by your own personal ZIP code!

CREATING A COUNTERFEIT CHRIST

**Looking
For
A
Messiah**

During World War 2, CBS correspondent William Shirer wrote in his Berlin Diary:

> I got my first glimpse of Hitler as he drove by the Würtemberger Hof to his own headquarters . . . I got caught in a mob of about 10,000 hysterics who jammed the moat in front of Hitler's hotel shouting, **"We want the Führer!"**
>
> I was literally shocked at the faces, especially those of the women.
>
> When Hitler finally appeared on the balcony for a moment . . . they looked at him as though he were the Messiah.

A rare and revealing photograph shows Adolf Hitler accepting a bouquet of roses from a child. Hitler knew how to appeal to the German people! And Antichrist will use the same techniques!

How did Hitler ever manage to rise in power in Germany? Is the United States caught in a pattern that will eventually produce a counterfeit Christ?

Germany fell in 1918 and World War 1 ended. But in 20 years history would repeat itself. Only this time, the remedy would be far more costly.

The Allied victors made the mistake at the Versailles Peace Conference to exact a tremendous price out of the Germans.

A man more subtle and more powerful than Hitler will arise!

The reparations bill imposed on the Germans was $132 Billion worth of gold or prewar currency called Marks. Remember, this was 1918 values ... not the 1980's inflated values. The debt seemed beyond hope of any payment.

From Comfort To Chaos

Germany was not only defeated but bankrupt! She never did pay that debt. The German Mark totally collapsed in 1923.

Before World War 1, the Mark was valued at about four to the dollar. By January, 1922 it took 160 Marks to make one dollar! During 1923 the Mark totally collapsed! It plunged from thousands to the dollar to millions and eventually trillions to equal just one dollar!

The middle class was completely wiped out! A family might use a lifetime of savings just for one meal! They were forced to sell the accumulated capital of several generations just for one warm coat!

Willard Cantelon, in his book, New Money Or None states:

> Elizabeth Kaatz, who served in a Berlin bank during those days of extreme inflation, said:
>
> > *People were bringing their money to the bank in cardboard boxes and laundry baskets ...*
> >
> > *We no longer counted the money; we merely put it on the scales and weighed it.*[1]

A spool of thread cost more in those

---

[1]Willard Cantelon, New Money Or None? (New Jersey: Logos International, 1979), p. 101.

Inflation Made A Hitler Possible!

What were the factors that made a Hitler possible?

1. The currency became worthless!
- Inflation is making the U.S. dollar lose much of its purchasing power!

2. $6 Billion in foreign loans collapsed!
- The United States gives some $10 Billion in foreign aid annually!

3. 6 Million Germans were unemployed!
- Today the United States has over 7 Million unemployed!

4. Unfair taxes, power of the great trusts, big money monopolies and power of the banks all were targets of Hitler's speeches!
- Today, the United States faces similar problems. AT&T earnings in 1980 hit an all time high ($6 Billion) while Exxon, the oil giant made 1980 profits of $5.66 Billion! These profits were earned while the average person struggled to pay soaring oil and gas bills and put food on their table!

tragic days than six new sewing machines had cost just 6 months before!

It was in this vacuum of total economic chaos that the people looked for a leader . . . a *"Messiah"* to give them a new birth. Born in Austria in 1889, Adolf Hitler suddenly became the shining star of Germany just 40 years later in 1929!

I'VE HEARD THAT SONG BEFORE!

A Convincing Speaker

Hitler used phrases we are familiar with today. Yet, as we look back on history, we can see that his definition of these words did not spell freedom but bondage!

Hitler called for a *"true democracy."* He declared that Germans must rely on themselves. He spoke out against Marxists, Bolsheviks, communists and socialists. He claimed the reason for the sorry condition of Germany was because of those who had received unearned incomes, war profits, and because of big business which created monopolies and interlocking trusts and unfair taxes!

If this sounds like familiar phrases . . . it is the same approach used by many leaders today. And Antichrist will use this same technique to inflame the public to support his request for total control of government — perhaps that of the United States!

A Possible Approach

Hitler was a master of oratory—so will Antichrist. But Antichrist will have a medium that Hitler did not have. Antichrist will be able to control the television waves!

ANTICHRIST . . .
A Persuasive Orator

What better way to stir a nation to action overnight! By way of prime time television he will plead:

> Give me your mandate to get government back on its feet again. Give me the power to restore the working class to dignity . . . to smash the selfish few who control the billion-dollar multinational businesses and whose only allegiance is to the making of more profits . . . at your expense.

> Let me put back nourishing food on your table so your child won't have to live on the edge of starvation!

> Let me put back dignity into your home . . . so your husband does not have to beg for meager wages!

> Let me put a roof over your head . . . that is a home and not a hovel! And one that you can pay off in a reasonable amount of time with a reasonable interest!

> Let me put a future into your life so you can see your sons and daughters live in a land of the free and the brave!

> I cannot do this if I must struggle through a government that is overgrown with weeds that strangle the very breath of progress . . . a government that feeds only its self-interests . . . and a 3 Million work force of federal employees who are leeching the very lifeblood of your happiness and future security!

> **I can only do this if you entrust me with ABSOLUTE POWER!**

> Give me this MANDATE and I will exercise this power as your faithful steward . . . slashing and cutting out the cancer of corruption so once again you can be proud . . . very proud that you are an AMERICAN!

Can you imagine what the results would be with such a stirring speech? As Hitler filled the void for a dying Germany . . . so Antichrist will be able to fill the void for Europe or United States on the brink of chaos!

THE COUNTERFEIT TRINITY

**The
New
Order**

The number **3** in Bible numerology is a number of action. And when Hitler gained the confidence of the German people he called his new order

The Third Reich

He declared that, following on the First Reich (the Holy Roman Empire), and the Second Reich (the Bismarck Empire), the Third Reich would carry on the process of true German history. Hitler prophesied that the Third Reich would last a thousand years! Reich means *"rule."* Today, it is obvious that the Third Reich did not last a thousand years. It lasted only 12 years!

**The
Soaring
Debt**

Look at the United States economy on a 3rd rule principle:

$1-Billion-a-Day President
It took 188 years . . . from George Washington to Jimmy Carter before a President was spending $1 Billion each day!

$2-Billion-a-Day President
It will take only 5 years . . . from Jimmy Carter to Ronald Reagan for a President to spend $2 Billion each day!

$3-Billion-a-Day President
In the 1985-1989 term, the then President will be spending $3 Billion for each day he is in office. Can it be that the man who is President at that time will be Antichrist? No one knows. Only time will tell!

**From
Hero
To
Tyrant!**

We do know, according to Scripture, that Antichrist will not be known as Antichrist until the middle of the 7-year Tribulation Period. It is at this time that he breaks his treaty with Israel and desecrates their Temple in Jerusalem!

Up until that time, the man, who eventually will be the tyrant Antichrist, may be the world's most popular figure. He will be eminently successful in solving the world's financial problems and in bringing peace between Arab nations and Israel! He will be the hero of heroes!

Adolf Hitler fades into insignificance when compared to the power, the prestige and the conquering passion of an Antichrist!

Hitler was the pattern that God allowed history to teach us.

The only problem is . . .

**we have learned nothing from history
. . . because we are not listening!**

9

MAKING MAN A CHEMICALLY CONTROLLED MACHINE

**The
Mark**

The Bible reveals that during the Tribulation Period that Antichrist:

> . . . causes all,
> the small and the great,
> and the rich and the poor,
> and the free man and the slaves,
> to be given a mark
> on their right hand,
> or on their forehead,
>
> and he provides that no one
> should be able to buy or to sell,
> except the one who has the mark,
> either the name of the beast
>   (Antichrist)
> or the number of his name.
>
> (Revelation 13:16-17)

We are further told that the number of his name is **666**.

The day will soon come when all hospitals will refuse admittance to a mother with a sick child because neither bears the Mark of Antichrist!

Subtle Force

**License
To
Live**

Now I am sure that not everyone living during this time will want to take on this Mark. But the coercive system at the time will compel masses to do so. When they see their children crying and then getting sick because of a lack of food; when they rush their children to the hospital and are turned away . . . such pressure will *"encourage"* them to give in and accept the Mark. It will be impossible to survive without this *"license to live."*

And by accepting the Mark they will take the first step in being reprogrammed into the mold that Antichrist desires.

People the world over, and particularly Americans, are already being conditioned for this new world system that will be under Antichrist. They may appear to be to you subtle little things that have no significance. But block upon block, they are stepping stones that are eventually paving the way for the Antichrist Mark on your right hand or forehead.

Destroying Identity

**Victims
Of
Progress**

Think how may things in your life have been reduced to numbers. Hitler knew that the first objective in brainwashing was to destroy a person's identity. The Nazis tatooed numbers on the arms of millions of Jews. They were forbidden to use their

**Holland
Citizens
Known To
Hitler!**

name. They had to use their number. This was the first step to whip them into submission and conformity.

This number became the universal identifier. Holland was proud of its super identification system it had installed prior to World War 2. Every citizen had a number. But France, easy going, kept very haphazard records of individuals . . . loose and slipshod.

What happened? When the Nazis invaded Holland they captured the files that contained the numbering codes and tracked down all the Jews in Holland. It was the numbers that led them to arrest the father of Anne Frank. Now, in France, it was a different matter. That is why many Jewish people fled to France for safety.

Trend Towards The Mark

Towns are now known by zip code. Phone exchanges are now numbers, not names. Products in supermarkets are now identified by a number and line marking system. The Government knows you by a number. Your most universal number is now your Social Security Number. Quite conceivably it could become the Mark. Technology is already here whereby the Social Security Number could be painlessly imprinted on your forehead or right hand in invisible ink revealed only by a special light.

The Government Computer

**You
Are
Marked**

The Internal Revenue Service has plans for the development of a nationwide $1 Billion computer for monitoring taxpayers. This massive data processing system with 8300 terminals would make it possible for some 48,300 IRS employees to have almost instantaneous access to the records of individuals and corporations.

In February, 1978, the Carter administration halted the plans for this computer giant because of opposition from Congress. However, one day, such a plan will become a reality.

World leaders whose ambition is for greater power know that if they can control the mind they can control the population. Russia has been moderately successful in this. But, unable to become completely successful, they have had to resort to crude force. They did this in Hungary. They did it in Berlin when they built the Berlin Wall.

Drugs Destroy Initiative

**A
Dangerous
Drug**

How can you control the mind? Their first step is to recognize that man can become a machine . . . a controlled machine through a chemical process. Valium is a typical example of a mood-changing drug. In 1980, doctors in the United States wrote approximately 80 million prescriptions for Valium and other mood-changing drugs, resulting in retail sales of over a billion dollars. Despite Valium's vast popularity, little is understood about how it works and even less about the condition it is taken to combat.

And This Is What You Put In Your Body!

Valium is made up of aniline which comes from nitrobenzene. Nitrobenzene is prepared by treating benzene with a mixture of nitric and sulfuric acids. The second component is benzoic acid which comes from toluene, a petroleum product. The third component is glycine, an amino acid. The fourth component is the addition of the methyl group, achieved by treating the compound with caustic soda and dimethylsulfate. The dimethylsulfate is obtained by treating chlorosulfonic acid with methyl alcohol, commonly known as wood alcohol. That is Valium! And in any given year, 20% of all American women and 14% of men will use the drug.

Continued use of tranquilizers can cause slow, rhythmic, involuntary movement of the tongue and facial muscles and uncontrolled movement of the arms, legs and trunk.

Depression Before Submission

A Subtle Approach

Whatever your personal opinion is about Valium, you can see that this and other mood changing drugs can work to the benefit of Antichrist. If he can get most of the population to forget about their troubles and struggle for living, by swallowing a pill, his battle is almost already won for complete dominance of the nations.

The brain has about 10 Billion working cells, which are called neurons. They weigh only six ounces! Anyone who can exercise some control over these *"action"* cells can control the human being! Mood changing drugs such as Valium depress these cells and give one *"the devil-may-care attitude."* They make one much more vulnerable to conformity.

Tranquilized Through Your Water

A Way To Control

This chemical control can also be added through our drinking water, without our knowledge. A population could be kept docile, and subjugated to the powers in control, by dosing the drinking water with a tranquilizing chemical.

Or they may wish to add some aggression-inciting chemical to the drinking water . . . or for that matter, even to the air we breathe!

Most people don't even know what is already in the water they drink! They would be surprised if they had it analyzed. Many communities have added fluorides to the water, as an example. This decision made by a few, is imposed on an entire community.

How easy, when a world leader wants to launch a massive propaganda campaign, for buckets of a specified chemical to be dumped in strategic water basins designed to produce the desired conforming effects! Fantasy? Absolutely not. Entirely possible today!

Why Tranquilizers

Walking Robots!

How many leaders can you count in your own church who are already taking tranquilizers and look like walking pill boxes? And yet we are the people who claim the Blessed Hope! We are the ones who should rest in God and cast all our burdens on Him. But, in reality, how many actually do that? Be honest. What about yourself? Do you find yourself dependent on drugs to give you a state of euphoria? Or do you look to the Saviour to give you peace of mind and freedom from fear? You may be surprised to find out how many Pastors are taking mood-changing drugs!

Now, what I am saying is this. If even Christians are hooked on mood-changing drugs, in spite of the hope that is within us through Jesus Christ, how much more widespread is the use of mood-changing drugs by those whose only hope is living for today!

What a tragic situation!

And what a ripe opportunity for Antichrist to make a man a chemically controlled machine, a slave to his whim and call, to do his bidding.

If the nation is already tranquilized . . . can the day of infamy be far behind?

10

THE DAY THEY
TRANSPLANT MEMORIES

**Memory
Transfers**

Some new discoveries have been made by psychologists regarding memory. This is another extension of the marking system. And these revelations have left many scientists alarmed because of the ulterior possibilities of controlling man.

When one begins to alter God's creation, man, through mood and mind control and manipulation of genes, one opens a literal Pandora's box.

You may remember the myth about a woman who, in curiosity, opened a box, letting out all human ills into the world.

You may remember the myth about a woman who, in curiosity, opened a box, letting out all human ills into the world.

We believe that our memories are personal. They are ours. They cannot be transferred. They are private.

Not so!

Scientists have discovered that memories can be transferred. This has already been accomplished in the animal world. And to accomplish this on humans is entirely within the realm of possibility . . . within the next 10 years!

One researcher experimented with the inch-long flatworm. Its brain has about 400 cells. They trained the worms to retract into an accordian shape whenever the light went on in their water tank.

The Cannibal Worms

Experiments Work

Those worms that were **trained** to coil upon a light signal were then fed to untrained, cannibal worms. Other cannibal worms were fed **un**trained flatworms. The cannibal worms that ate trained flatworms exhibited the same reflex behavior when the light was turned on. Memory transfer was working.

Then researchers began working with rats to see if their memories could be transferred to hamsters; thus breaking the species barrier!

They educated the rats and mice to shun darkness. Now rats and mice normally prefer darkness. But they were trained in a reversal technique. Much of this training was done through shock treatments using the Russian Pavlov basic data that was gathered from experiments on dogs many years ago.

Crossing The Species

After the rats and mice were trained, their brains were removed and made into a souplike consistency and injected into hamsters. Soon the injected hamsters began to shun darkness! Memory had been transferred this time across species!

Scientists were further intrigued. What specific substance was the key that triggered the brain to accept transfer of memory? One scientist finally isolated this substance which he called scotophobin (Greek for *fear of darkness*).

We are already witnessing subtle methods of mind manipulation.

The Peptide Discovery

Making Memory Banks!

In further tests some 4000 conditioned rats were killed and their brains were converted to a soupy substance so that an isolation of the triggering molecules could be achieved. What they came up with was **peptide**. Peptide is a complex amino acid sequence.

Since then several other brain peptides have been discovered.

What are the implications from this research? If these peptides can be synthesized, a large number of *"memories"* can be manufactured as easily as one makes a hammer or nail. Synthesize means that these *"memory banks"* can be created by man without having to extract them from animals. Many more possibilities can be achieved if peptide can be created in the drug laboratories.

Peptide injections could replace school textbooks, as an example. A student would simply receive an injection that would transfer to him the memory of a scholar or genius.

Tragic Future

More sinister, peptide injections could be used to indoctrinate individuals to a passive nature with a *"Casper Milktoast"* personality. A dictator, such as Antichrist, could make much use of a memory exchange bank. He could take the memory of an electronic or space age genius who was uncooperative and inject the memory into a cooperative but average intelligent follower.

He could inject peptides of murderers and lawless individuals into his entire army and add a peptide that would give them suicidal tendencies in combat ... dying without fear for their master.

But there's more!

Not only is it possible to transfer memory ... but a number of tests have indicated that it is also possible to **prevent memory storage!**

Memory Erasers

Frightening Possibilities

Scientists in using the antibiotic drug called puromycin have been able to actually **erase** memory in tests with animals. What a boon this would be in the hands of Antichrist. I often wondered how those living in the Tribulation Period would follow Antichrist and would not want to turn to Christ. Now Scriptures do tell us that they will be under a strong delusion and will believe a lie.

But may it also be possible that Antichrist may exercise a "memory eraser" on some uncooperative individuals?

Suppose the Rapture were to occur tomorrow and the Tribulation Period of 7 years were to begin in a month or two. All the people living would have a knowledge of religion. A vast majority of Americans as well as others throughout the world would have a knowledge of the Bible. Millions would remember the evangelistic campaigns of yesterday. There would still

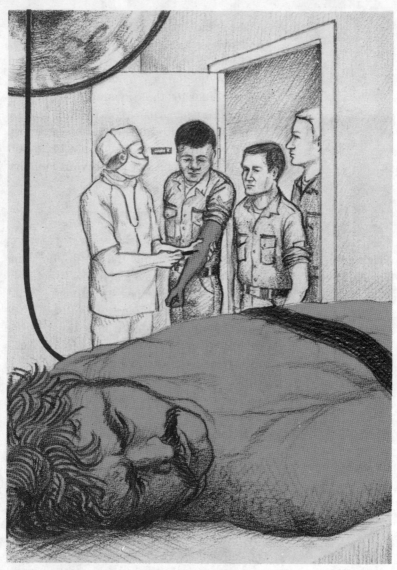

Antichrist, using memory transfer techniques, could order the injection of peptides from murderers and lawless individuals into his entire army to make them aggressive and ruthless.

The Awesome Results!

be millions of Christian books and Bibles which would reveal exactly what is happening in the Tribulation.

Certainly some, maybe millions would awaken to the fact of their dilemma! And here is where this drug would be useful. Suppose it were administered through the water systems. Or suppose special aircraft were sent aloft to seed the atmosphere.

In drinking the water or breathing the air, individuals would unknowingly have certain parts of their memory storage banks erased and their minds would be highly susceptible to new thoughts and ideas.

Highly populated areas such as India could be given an extra dose that would stunt their mental capacities. They would become the menial labor force of the world.

Frightening, isn't it? And it seems untrue. Perhaps right now you are reading this with much skepticism and telling yourself, *"It will never happen!"*

May I suggest you take the time to research the facts, as I have done. Then you will realize why it is so important for us to double our efforts to reaching the lost now . . . and reorganizing our priorities.

It is now possible to transfer memories. And it is now possible to erase memories.

And when Antichrist enters the scene, you can be assured he will make use of every devious device to achieve his desired goal of world domination. What are you doing about it . . . right now?

11

YOUR FOOD PURCHASES ARE CONTROLLED

Electronic Scanners

The first step towards controlling your purchasing of food has **already** been initiated!

At a faster pace than ever before ... supermarkets are installing **electronic scanners** at their checkout counters!

Supermarkets had their birth in the early 1930's. By January, 1940 there were over 6000 supermarkets nationwide. By 1950 this figure had zoomed to over 14,000. In 1960, more than 33,000 supermarkets emerged. Now there are over 50,000!

Some 1.4 Million Americans are on the supermarket payroll. That's why in the last 10 years labor costs in supermarkets have climbed 171%. Seeking an answer, the supermarkets are now installing electronic price scanners. Even though it costs some

$100,000 per store for this laser beam system, it cuts costs, increases profits. (The average supermarket, after taxes, makes a net profit of less than one cent per dollar of sales).

UNIVERSAL PRODUCT CODE

**You
Can Be
Manipulated**

UPC is the abbreviation for *"Universal Product Code."* This is a universal coding system used throughout the United States by most manufacturers.

The series of bars, lines and numerals provide identifying marks.

The series of lines and 5 numerals on the left identify the manufacturer or distributor.

The lines and 5 numerals on the right identifies a specific product and its size.

The price of the item is **NOT** contained in the UPC symbol nor in the numerals. The current price is in the computer!

There is a familiar computer saying:

Put garbage into the computer and you will get garbage out of the computer.

What this means is this . . . the computer is a slave to its human master! What the computer operator punches into the computer by way of information . . . the computer will automatically read out.

Recently, I recall, going to a supermarket where the Laser Pricing Unit was in operation. The cashier passed the product over

The automatic scanner pictured above automatically reads the Universal Product Code. As the product is passed over the plate, a laser beam shines in all directions through the **X** opening. What the customer cannot see is the warning label that appears underneath this **X** plate. It reads: DIRECT LASAR RADIATION. Years from now we will learn it caused cancer in those we love . . . including our children!

the laser beam. The beam dutifully read the Universal Product Code (UPC). This was instantly passed on to the central control computer and the price relayed back to the cash register. All this occurs within a split instant.

I looked at the price as registered on the customer screen. It was obvious I was being overcharged for that item. I called this to the attention of the cashier. She also recognized this and corrected the error.

What I am saying is this . . . it is possible for the computer operator at central control to push the wrong price data for a particular product. As an example . . . a 16 ounce can of Del Monte Stewed Tomatoes that should sell for 59¢ could have the figures transposed to 95¢!

Thus the "garbage" punched into the computer . . . because of a transposing error . . . makes you the victim by an overcharge.

THE INCH CONCEPT

I am sure you remember the phrase, "Give them an inch and they'll take a yard."

At present, one insurance shoppers have is that prices still are on the products themselves. But there is a trend and pressure to do away with individual product pricing . . . simply placing the price on the shelf.

This would give way to the possibility of the Inch Concept. A supermarket owner could instruct his computer operator to

**Undetected
Inflation**

"inch up" on product prices. The "inching" would be done by simply punching in an **additional PENNY** to the price of fast moving products.

Thus, automatically, as volumes of these products pass through the laser beam, it picks up a new price which adds additional profits to the store and subtracts dollars from your purchasing power ... without you realizing it!

The new cash register tape via the scanning device gives you more detailed information ... but how many people actually take time to read food tapes!

HOW THE SCANNER WORKS

The laser beam emits its light and reads the Universal Product Code. The amazing thing is that this beam emerges from its source ... **in all directions!** Thus, the product does not have to be held in any certain way to be read by the computer. Since it does emit its beam in all directions ... you, invariably, are being penetrated with this beam also.

No one knows the ultimate dangers of this laser beam. It is known that the laser destroys skin pigments. Years from now, we may discover that our children have a higher incidence of cancer or mental retardation! Time will tell!

12

THE SILENT DEATH OF THE SMALL FARMER

Americans . . . used to shopping at their local supermarket and buying anything they want . . . are in for a rude shock!

What you may not realize is that over the past 30 years there have been drastic changes in our farming landscape! These changes will eventually pave the way for Antichrist to institute a **Marking** system. Part of the reason given will be so that everyone may secure a fair share of the available limited quantities of food!

Anyone who is familiar with the statistics can realize that:

    A. The population of the United States is growing. From 230 Million in 1981 . . . it will double to over 400 million within 20 years!

    B. At the same time that our population is mushrooming . . . our available farmland is DECREASING!

Unfortunately, people from all over the world are relying on bountiful harvests from the United States. People in India,

Africa, South America are not looking for any luxuries but merely food enough to keep them from starving!

> In 1940, there were almost 7 million farms in the United States. Today there are only 2 million!

> In 1940, some 30 million persons were engaged in farming. Today there are less than 6 million!

Farming Controlled By A Few!

Farming is no longer controlled by the small, independent farmer, either! Today the majority of farm operations are controlled by big business!

How many Americans know, for example, that a conglomerate, International Telephone and Telegraph owns Wonder bread, Hostess Twinkies, Burpee Seeds! The A & P supermarkets are owned by a German conglomerate! Grand Union stores are owned by a British conglomerate! Foreign money is flooding the United States and more and more U.S. companies are now controlled by foreign firms.

In 1966, direct foreign investments in the United States totaled only $9 Billion. But look at this ... right now foreign investments annually total over $70 BILLION!

Food To The Highest Bidder

When food shortages begin to appear shortly ... do you think these foreign-owned U.S. farmlands and food processors will channel all the food into U.S. supermarkets? **Not on your life!** There will be

**Sympathy
Does Not
Make Profits!**

such a demand for the available food that foreign countries will offer a higher price.

These foreign-based investors will sell the food wherever they can make the biggest profit! They have no allegiance to the United States. They are multi-national (or international) in their allegiance. When the time comes that food is at a premium . . . they will not show any sympathy. They wouldn't even give food to their own grand-

SEVERE SHRINKAGE IN WORLD GRAIN RESERVES

Total World Grain Reserves

In 1972

209 million
metric tons—or
enough to feed
the world's
population for

66
days

In 1981

44 million
metric tons—
enough to feed
the world's
population for

14
days

Note: Reserves include grain that could be produced on idle cropland. Copyright © 1981, Salem Kirban, Inc.

mother . . . if they can make a profit selling it elsewhere!

**Paved
With
Concrete**

Coupled with this, the agriculture business (agribusiness) employs more than 20% of American workers and accounts for about 20% of consumer expenditures!

With farm land decreasing many farm workers will be out of jobs! This will add to the crisis! We are already losing some 3 million acres of land a year in the U.S. In the name of progress . . . most of it is paved over with concrete!

THE SOIL CRISIS

**Soil
Becoming
Barren**

In the last two centuries, America has lost at least one-third of its topsoil. In the state of Washington, as an example, 20 pounds of topsoil are washed away for every pound of wheat that's grown! In Pennsylvania, the production of one bushel of corn results in the erosion of five bushels of soil.

At the present rate of $1000 per acre for cropland . . . it is estimated that $4.5 Billion worth of soil disappears each year! And this soil cannot be replaced overnight. Nature requires 200 to 3000 years just to manufacture one inch of topsoil!

It was Franklin Roosevelt who said:

*The nation that destroys its soil
destroys itself!*

THE WATER CRISIS

**Water
Is
Polluted**

In the 1930's irrigation began in the vast arid areas of the Mid and Southwest. The parched land came to life as fossil water thousands of years old was discovered underground. Experts estimate that there is only about 20 years left of this useable water.

We are rapidly draining every available resource to produce food. Soon we will hit rock bottom!

THE FERTILIZER CRISIS

**Depletion
Of
Resources**

The life blood of modern farming is cheap fertilizer. There has been production of synthetic nitrogen fertilizer, called urea. But this consumes huge quantities of natural gas. But by 1990 the price of gas will be so high that it will not be feasible to use it to manufacture fertilizer.

The U.S. supply of phosphorus and potassium, crucial to farming, will be depleted within 20 years! And yet we are sending

Look at the photograph to the right. Notice the anguish on the face of this Japanese woman. What is causing this anguish? You will be shocked and surprised when you find out and see the rest of this photograph! The full photo and explanation appear on page 96.

IT TAKES FEWER AND FEWER YEARS TO ADD A BILLION TO THE WORLD'S POPULATION

World population reached 1 billion people in 1830. Since then—

• If the population explosion goes unchecked, experts at the United Nations say, the number of people in the world will nearly triple—reaching 11.2 billion—by the year 2050.

• If the world's nations adopt a policy of "zero population growth," population will keep on expanding for decades—though at a much slower rate—before leveling off. Under one timetable prepared by a leading U.S. economist, world population would stabilize at just under 6 billion people by the year 2015.

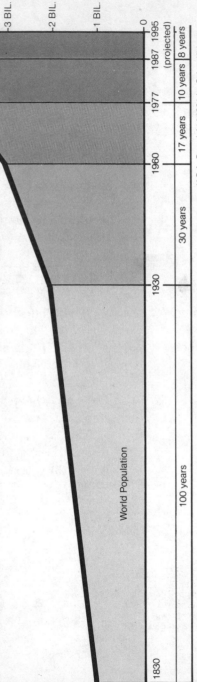

World Population

1830	1930	1960	1977	1987	1995
100 years	30 years	17 years	10 years	8 years	(projected)

6 BIL. / 5 BIL. / 4 BIL. / 3 BIL. / 2 BIL. / 1 BIL. / 0

the Soviet Union almost 3 million metric tons of phosphate each year, **and our trade agreement guarantees this shipment annually for the next 20 years!**

Dead Sea . . .
Trigger
For
War!

The last remaining frontier for fertilizer will be the **DEAD SEA!** Now does it all add up to you? The nations of the world will converge on Israel to capture the rich mineral content of the Dead Sea. That is why we will soon witness Russia maneuvering to conquer Israel. That is why Antichrist will make Israel his prime target for conquest! There will be a desperate struggle for survival as food becomes a premium. The Dead Sea will be like a tantalizing dinner to a starving, hungry man. The nations of the world will yet rush to devour this resource!

THE FOOD TRANSPORTATION CRISIS

The Day
Your
Supermarket
Closes!

The shipping of food across country eats up more fuel than any other industry. Annually the U.S. food system uses some 500 million gallons of fuel.

Look at this! Last year, New Yorkers bought 24,000 tons of broccoli. Most of it was purchased from California . . . some 2700 miles away at a cost of $6 Million! And this same procedure is followed for some 11 other fresh vegetables. For every $2 that is spent to grow food . . . another $1 goes to ship it!

There is such a demand for food today in the United States that there is only about a two week backlog of storage! Think about

**Enter
The
Marking
System**

this for a moment. If the Teamsters suddenly strike ... if the Persian Gulf closes ... the food industry would just about come to a standstill. Supermarket shelves would quickly empty. Hoarding and panic would ensue! Riots and civilian unrest would bring in the army.

Eventually we would become a controlled country headed by a benevolent dictatorship. A world leader could then institute a distribution system for food which would have as its prime force a Marking system on your right hand or forehead! This could well be the way THE MARK makes its entrance into our economy!

By that time half the population would be on food stamps. A single loaf of bread would cost $8. Three tomatoes could cost $5. And a 10-ounce jar of instant coffee (if you could find it) would cost $45!

This is what happens when shortages occur! This scene, in a Japanese supermarket, will happen here shortly.

What are these Japanese housewives scrambling for? It's located in the lower left portion of the photograph! Toilet Tissue!

13

NO MAN MAY BUY

The Tragic End

In Revelation 13:16, 17 . . . we are told that the False Prophet, in the Tribulation Period will make it mandatory that everyone be given a Mark on their right hand or on their forehead.

> . . . and he provides
> that no one
> should be able to BUY . . .
> except the one
> who has the Mark!
>
> (Revelation 13:17)

The year 1980 saw a rapid increase in the number of **Laser Scanning Devices** being installed in supermarkets. Although this device has been available for years . . . it met with consumer resistance. Suddenly consumers are accepting what supermarkets have called a *"marketing miracle."*

But one must remember this. While the Laser Scanning Device, in conjunction with the Universal Product Code, may lower food prices (and this is doubtful), it will also be the capstone to controlling YOU!

How this event may occur. These illustrations are from **666 Pictorial** by Salem Kirban. If you wish this book, send $4 to: Salem Kirban, Inc., Kent Road, Huntingdon Valley, Penna. 19006. Price includes postage and handling.

**To Avoid
A
Stampede!**

Project yourself 20 or 30 years from now. Increasing population ... less available farmland ... more pollution ... and much greater demand for food products ... that's the scene! With twice as many people living in the United States, they will want to shop at their supermarket for food. How will this stampede be averted with too many people and shortages of basic foods?

Rationing And Zoning Shopping Plan

First, the government will issue a **rationing and zoning shopping plan.**

You will be told that each person can buy a certain quantity of specified foods per week.

You will also be told that these purchases must be made in the supermarkets located in your immediate *"food-zoned"* area.

Now, here comes the punch line!

You will be told that in order for this system to work efficiently and fairly ... each person must have a foolproof identifying MARK!

The MARK will be a *"harmless"* and *"invisible"* Laser Beam applied mark. You will have the choice of having the Mark placed either on your right hand or on your forehead!

The newspapers will be primed for this big event. It will be termed the *"patriotic thing to do!"* Liberals and left-wing conservationists will hail this new plan! Newspapers will carry photos of the President becoming the first citizen to have his Mark applied!

The Velvet Glove

To further their point . . . the media will be given photos showing a little baby with the Mark. She will be sitting at the supermarket cash register as the beam reveals her number. The caption will read something like this.

> *Under the Laser Beam Scanning System . . . even your child will get his fair share of food. Register for your identifying Food Purchase Mark today. It's the patriotic thing to do! And it will assure your family of the nourishing food to which you are entitled! Be part of the Team! Get on the BEAM!*

Anyone who refuses to go along with this Marking device will be considered both an outcast and unpatriotic . . . a detriment to society.

A SIGN OF THE FUTURE?

All of us are familiar with the <u>Universal Product Codes</u> (UPC) that appear on our food packages. They are a series of long vertical marks of various widths!

However, the technology is already here to add another series of small lines at the bottom of each code . . . perhaps a 7, 8, 9 line series with an **F** *(to stand for forehead)* in the front and an **H** *(to stand for hand)* at the back. Be alert and be wise as serpents!

A symbol <u>similar</u> to this has already appeared on fig bar packages in some Midwest supermarkets.

**The
Anti-Christian
Movement**

As food becomes even scarcer there will even be a more tragic trend of events! The elections of 1980 will be remembered as the turning point of conflict! Conservative Christian groups became active in electing a President. They became highly vocal in their anti-abortion and moral majority stands. They made the front covers of national magazines and prime time television.

This gave birth to a Christian backlash as liberals invested millions of dollars to undermine Christians who stood on the Word of God!

The continuing pressures of Christian conservative groups will eventually polarize the liberals into action. Eventually, the liberal establishment will regain control of government.

It must be remembered that Satan is
". . . the prince of this world"
(John 12:31; 14:30; 16:11) . . . and also of this evil world-system which he has organized upon his own principles (2 Corinthians 4:3-4).

Despite the efforts of religious political action groups . . . Satan will not experience any defeat until the end of the Tribulation Period at the Battle of Armageddon. And his final downfall will not come until the end of the 1000 year Millennium!

In one sense, religious political action groups become pawns in the hands of Satan. They help polarize Christians against non-Christians.

**The
Backlash
Has
Started**

TWO GROUPS

There are many who condone Christian political activists groups. They believe that we should stand up and be counted and *". . . not let the liberals run all over us."* Those who hold this opinion are sincere Christians with dedicated goals.

On the other hand, there is a large body of Christians who believe our primary purpose is to preach the Gospel and win souls to Christ. They believe you cannot legislate morality . . . that one must first change the heart. They believe that infiltration of the enemy camp by the preaching of the Gospel is more effective than blasting the enemy camp through enforced legislation.

PERSECUTION OF CHRISTIANS TO COME

Regardless of what position you favor . . . the Christian activist or Gospel-centered Christian . . . believers will face increasing persecution.

And that persecution will be triggered because Christian political activists have lit a fire under godless liberals throughout the country. Suddenly these liberals are unifying in a concentrated effort to squash anything that smacks of Bible fundamentalism!

In control of all this backlash action is SATAN!

**Food
Shortage
To Trigger
Persecution**

All of that is said to say this!

As the population doubles from its present 230 Million in the United States to some 400 Million by the year 2000 . . . critical problems will arise.

The major problem will be food!

As we mentioned earlier . . . the Government will institute a Rationing and Zoning Plan. Those living at that time will be allocated a specific quantity of each type of food. They will only be able to buy that food in the supermarket in their Living Zone area! The control will be the Laser Beam at your supermarket cash register. It will "read out" the back of your hand or forehead to

    (A) See if you are allowed your allotment or whether you have already used up your food allotment for that week . . . and

    (B) See if you are shopping in your approved Food Zone Area.

**A
Possible
Approach**

THE NEXT STEP as times become progressively worse will be to blame the reason for these food shortages on Christians. You may see an article like this in your newspaper or hear a TV newscaster say:

> The President acknowledged today in a worldwide press conference that the tragic food shortages we are experiencing can be directly related to so-called "born again" Christians who have taken the book of Genesis seriously.

During the famine in China, people standing in line were shoving and pushing hoping to retrieve just a scrap of left-over food.

**Christians
Blamed!**

The President quoted Genesis 1:28 and said religionists have worked this verse to death. The verse: *"Be fruitful and multiply, and fill the earth, and subdue it."*

The President, with anger visibly rising, commented that in the 1980's religious political activists protested abortions and by their own lifestyle subdued the earth. He continued:

Throughout history Christians and the Saviour they hold so dearly have caused nothing but tears and tragedy for all of us.

Today we find ourselves over-populated, unable to adequately feed our very own children. We find our land . . . once bountiful and green . . . paved over with industry and barren!

Therefore, I issue this edict to become law as **Presidential Order #666.**

Anyone not bearing a laser beam identifiable Mark either on their forehead or the back of their right hand will **not** be able to purchase food in their Zoned area supermarket.

This should separate those who name the name of any other Master from those whose allegiance is to their country and its leader!

While these are drastic measures . . . I am sure you will agree with me . . . that if you and your treasured children are to receive even the barest of sustenance, then food must be rationed and even denied to those who will not cooperate — whose previous actions have brought us to the crisis we face today!

**Looking
Back
To
Look
Ahead**

Now as you read this it may seem far out and unbelievable. But this was written in 1981. I challenge you to read this in the year 2000 and see how believable suddenly it will become.

Or look back 20 years!

Who would have thought 20 years ago that a laser beam would read the price of the products you buy and automatically register the amount on the cash register?

Who would have believed 20 years ago that you could buy a watch in Hong Kong and within a split second . . . your credit would be approved or denied by a computer based in Atlanta, Georgia!

Who would have believed 20 years ago that through an electronic beam from Iran bounced off a satellite back to the U.S. . . . you could actually witness the release of 52 hostages as it happened!

That day is rapidly approaching when NO man will be able to buy or sell unless he has the approved Mark of Antichrist! **The technology is already here!** And that man . . . Antichrist . . . may also already be here . . . waiting in the wings . . . for the proper time to make his entrance!

14

THE
HAND-SCAN
MACHINE

**Ready
To
Identify
Your
Mark!**

Various methods of identification are being tested by the international banking community.

The simplest one would be the *"Smart"* credit card with its electronic memory chip.

But it is important that the one using the card is the actual owner of that card authorized to use it.

Therefore, banks are working on other means of identifying the user. One of those means is the **Hand-Scan machine.**

Tests are now going on in which this scanning machine is being used. You place your hand on a plate. This scanning device measures every mark on the palm of your hand.

Through the electronic hook-up through master control, your palm print is identified and verified . . . instantly!

The HAND SCAN Machine

**Hand Scan Machine
Checks
Individual Identity**

There already has been developed an unusual machine which provides quick identification.

In the coming "cashless society," it will be absolutely essential that the dispensers of goods and services be able to quickly and positively identify those who offer credit cards and checks in payment. A manufacturing Company in Connecticut has developed an electronic machine that, unattended and automatically, performs verification with what is described as scientific accuracy.

Identity of the prospective purchaser or check-casher is established by the geometry of a person's hand. A person granted a credit card, check-cashing ID card, security pass, etc., puts his right hand into the Identimat device (photo) that mechanically measures the geometry of the hand and reduces these unique measurements to an electronic code (magnetic or optical markings) which are placed in the individual's credit or ID card.

When the card bearer goes shopping, he establishes his credit by placing both his card and right hand into the Identimat which electronically compares the two and lights up an "accept" button, signifying the person is who the card says he is. The machine will lease for about $15 a month.

One can see how such a machine could be used by Antichrist in the Tribulation Period.

Many businessmen have privately stated that such a course of unifying world finance would be more than welcome!

**Controlled
By
Your Own
Hand!**

The Hand-Scan machine could replace the credit card. The machine can *"read"* your right hand and assign you a credit number. When you go to the bank, you dial this number ... press your hand to the machine and it unlocks your account. Such a device is less costly than a *"Smart"* credit card. While a *"Smart"* credit card can be stolen or manipulated ... your palm print is not only accurate but a sure, safe identification system!

**A
Sudden Rise
In
Home Gardens**

Many would decide to have their own family garden behind their home. But this would be impossible. Thieves would steal the produce as soon as it was matured!

Thus we see available farm land decreasing ...

    most food output controlled
        by large international conglomerates
    dwindling soil, water, fertilizer
        which makes for
    lower yield of food products
        and
        higher prices!

All this adds to eventual chaotic times, a military government control and a Marking system that will exclude anyone who names the name of Christ!

It was Reginald McKenna (Britain's Chancellor of the Exchequer) who said in 1915:

*They who control the credit of a nation
direct the policy of the government
and hold in the hollow of their hands
the destiny of the people!*

**Confirming
Allegiance**

One can see how Revelation 13:15-18 is already coming into possibility. Everyone will have to have a mark on their right hand or on their forehead. This identifying system will confirm allegiance to Antichrist.

**Six
Facts**

We are told **six** basic facts regarding the Mark of Revelation 13:

1. To receive the Mark . . . each person will have to worship its image.
2. Those who refuse to worship the image of Antichrist will be killed.
3. No matter what position in society nor whether rich or poor . . . all will have to receive the Mark in order to function!
4. The total economy will center around the Mark. No buying or selling can be done without it!
5. The Mark is not a credit card . . . so you won't receive it by accident or have it mailed to you. It will be a permanent marking system placed on the right hand or forehead.
6. By receiving the Mark, you will automatically doom yourself to an eternity in Hell. See Revelation 19:20, 21.

The Mark could be painlessly administered to you by a laser beam. Quite possibly this Mark will be invisible to the human eye but legible under the designated scanning light.

15

CONTROLLING THE CHRISTIANS

Tiny Transmitters Bring Terror

In the Tribulation Period there will be other ways besides the Laser Beam MARK to control the Christians.

These security devices already exist and, in fact, are being used today by both business and government!

Security companies now offer such devices as computerized voice and fingerprint identification systems. They also have tiny transmitters that can be imbedded beneath the skin of potential kidnap victims and video cameras that can fit inside a shirt pocket.

**No
Place
To
Hide!**

All those in the Tribulation Period who refuse to take the Mark could have a tiny transmitter implanted in their body. Such a transmitter could not only map and identify the movements of that individual but perform a host of other spy services. This transmitter chip . . . smaller than a dime . . . could serve as a microphone and transmit everything you say back to a central control station. It could even monitor your emotions and thought processes. With a little more sophistication, it could even influence your behavior making you subservient to Antichrist!

In 1972 the security business in minicomputer spy devices was a $2 Billion business. Today it is over a $15 Billion business!

Fingermatrix, Inc. makes a fingerprint scanner. At present this scanner device costs $50,000 for the minicomputer plus $10,000 for each access terminal.

YOUR OWN PERSONAL ZIP CODE

Then, too, the Post Office is introducing a 9-digit ZIP code. This adds initially 20 million more zip codes areas. But, more important, this 9-digit ZIP code gives the U.S. Postal Service the mathematical possibility of making up nearly 1 billion codes. **This comes out to about four code numbers for every person in the United States!**

Tied into government computers such an extensive ZIP code system could rapidly identify and control each individual through an assigned number. In the hands of Antichrist . . . such a number could be assigned as simply an apparent individualized mail code *"to give each person better service."* Realistically, however, it could become an identifying code you would use to buy or sell!

Soon
A
Reality!

And for believers . . . it could become a way of controlling those who do not swear allegiance to Antichrist!

Right now it may seem like fiction. But it is already within the realm of becoming a reality!

Sterilizing retarded OKd

Up to courts, not parents, N.J. justices rule

Bulletin Wire Services

TRENTON — The state Supreme Court ruled yesterday that the mentally incompetent can be sterilized if the courts determine that preventing them from having children is in their best interest.

The unanimous decision is the first to set guidelines for the sterilization of the mentally retarded in New Jersey.

The ruling came in the case of 19-year-old Lee Ann Grady, of Sparta, Sussex County.

In 1979, Superior Court Judge Bertram Polow granted Miss Grady's parents, Edward and Luann Grady, the right to choose sterilization as a way to control the sexuality they said their daughter did not understand.

The high court vacated that decision, however, saying authorization for such a procedure rests with the courts. The justices sent the case back to the lower court with a set of strict standards that the judge must consider in reaching his decision.

In an opinion written by Justice Morris Pashman, the court said Polow omitted several considerations in issuing his ruling, including contraceptive alternatives to sterilization and the psychological impact of the procedure on Miss Grady.

The high court said it used the individual's constitutional right to privacy as the basis for its ruling that courts, not parents, are empowered to authorize sterilization.

The individual's constitutional right to privacy was the same consideration it employed five years ago in deciding the landmark case of Karen Ann Quinlan, a comatose woman.

The court authorized her removal from life-support apparatus because she was unable to decide for herself.

". . . (U)ltimately we decided that the patient's constitutional right of privacy outweighed the public interest in preserving her life and presented compelling judicial intervention. Similar compelling considerations exist in the present case," the court said.

Lee Ann suffers from Down's Syndrome and was determined to be mentally incompetent.

New laws are slowly taking away the rights of parents over their children. this is a sign of the End Times!

NO PLACE TO HIDE

Antichrist's TRACKING DEVICE ...
A Human Transponder!

In January, 1971, the details of a plan to track human beings was revealed in *Transactions on Aerospace and Electronics Systems* magazine.

The computer specialist who developed this human tracking device calls it the

Crime Deterrent Transponder System

This was developed by the National Security Agency, the U.S. Government secret intelligence organization. It is part of the Pentagon's Peacefare program.

The Crime Deterrent Transponder System is a scheme for attaching miniature electronic devices to criminals or other suspect citizens and keeping track of them by computer!

A Transponder is an electronic device that emits radio or radar signals in response to pulses received.

The plan was initially to attach this *"spy"* device to 2 million *"subscribers"* as a condition of bail or parole. Each individual would be identified by a unique code. This code would be transmitted several times a minute to a computer by way of a network of electronic receivers. These sending devices could be built into police call-boxes.

The computer would record the individual's location ... compare it with a stored file that would *"specify the normal schedule for the individual including any territorial or curfew restrictions."*

If the computer found the individual to be in violation of these restrictions ... it would instruct the transponder (miniature electronic device) to warn its wearer of a violation.

These transponders could not be removed without the computer knowing it and alerting security forces. In this way, the computer would effectively control the lives of the persons plugged into it.

More sophisticated surveillance of every individual with a transponder device is now possible using spy satellites to transmit data instantly to a central master computer.

Credit for making this information known goes to Ron J. Steele of Christian Cable Communications.

16

THE MARK
AND
THE SEAL

**Jews
Sealed
By
God**

In the first 3½ years of the Tribulation Period, Revelation chapter 7 tells us that some Jews will receive a protective seal from God. This is in contrast to the Mark imposed by Antichrist in order to buy or to sell. In the case of the Mark, those who refuse to accept it, both Jew and Gentile alike, will suffer and many will die.

But between the breaking of the Sixth Seal and the Seventh Seal judgments, right after vast earthquakes occur and meteors fall to earth . . . we see an interval of time.

This will be a time in which 144,000 of the children of Israel, 12,000 from each of the 12 tribes, will be *"sealed."*

**A Seal
Of
Protection**

While the Mark of Antichrist will be either on the hand or forehead, God will place this seal of protection on their foreheads (Revelation 7:3).

> And I saw another angel
> ascending from the rising of the sun,
> having the seal of the living God;
> and he cried out with a loud voice
> to the four angels
> to whom it was granted
> to harm the earth and the sea,
> saying,
> "Do not harm the earth or the sea
> or the trees,
> until we have sealed the bond-servants
> of our God on their foreheads."
>
> And I heard the number of those
> who were sealed,
> one hundred and forty-four thousand
> sealed from every tribe of the
> sons of Israel.
>
> (Revelation 7:2-4)

One-Fourth Of Population Die

**Chosen
Witnesses**

This seal, as described in the verse just quoted, will be the mark of God and will identify them as God's chosen witnesses during the Tribulation Period. The amazing thing is that neither Antichrist nor the False Prophet nor Satan will be able to stop them from witnessing to their faith in Christ.

There will not be one Gentile in these 144,000! **They will all be Jews.** As to their actual identity, as far as the present is concerned, no one knows who they will be. But God will know who they are even though they may now be scattered among the nations.

Witness Prior To Exodus

It is quite conceivable that they will witness to the millions of Jews in the Holy Land and throughout the world just prior to the exodus of the Jews from Jerusalem. Let's take a moment to set the scene.

Just prior to God placing His seal on the 144,000, the Fourth Seal of judgment has just been released. This is a judgment of death which includes war, famine and disease. We are told in Revelation 6:7-8 that as a result of this judgment one-fourth of the population of the land will be destroyed!

> If the word *"land"* (or *"earth"*) refers to the entire globe, and if we went on the basis of our present population . . . this would mean that some 1 billion people or more will die through various judgments at this time! It may, however, only refer to Eurasia or to Palestine. In any case there will be mass death.

THE NEW YORK TIMES, FRIDAY, MAY 1, 1970

Christianity Linked to Pollution

By EDWARD B. FISKE
Special to The New York Times

CLAREMONT, Calif., April 30 —A group of Protestant theologians asserted here today that Christianity had played its part in provoking the current environmental crisis and that any solution to it would

Scholars Cite Call in Bible for Man to Dominate Life

major paper of the conference. "Individually and collectively we should rapidly

be the object of the same love that is directed to human beings.

The theologian said that because it was impossible for people to "believe something simply because it seems advantageous to believe it" a change

More and more you will see Christianity and Christians blamed for the ills of the world. Persecution will follow.

CHRISTIANS TO BE BLAMED

**Believers
To
Suffer**

Right after this catastrophe, undoubtedly many will blame these judgments on the Christians. This is not new. During the ecology campaigns of the late 1960's and early 1970's several pro-ecology writers blamed the ills of the world on the verse in Genesis 1:28 which says:

> . . . and God said to them, "Be fruitful and multiply and fill the earth, and subdue it . . ."

In effect, they said that Christians were to blame for the world conditions of today. They argued that Bible believers were only concerned with *"subduing"* the earth, and that they did not have any concern with preserving the earth.

Such accusations, during this Tribulation Period will, of course, be magnified particularly in light of the fact that believers will refuse to accept the Mark of Antichrist.

As a result, in the breaking of the Fifth Seal judgment we find many, many believers martyred (Revelation 6:9-11). Such martyrdom may well come in the form of beheading. Seeing, how in the future Antichrist will desecrate the Temple of the Jews, it would not be surprising if such mass beheadings took place right on Church lawns in front of thousands of spectators, as an example to others! See Revelation 20:4 which reveals that many believers, because of their testimony, will be beheaded!

ABIDING LOVE/ Goodbye My Sweetheart for just tonight, May God watch o'er you till morning light. From Heaven above, you'll find me waiting. With joy I'll sing my song of love. (This song Bill Sanders sings to his wife, Faye, in the book **666***, when he is led into the guillotine.)

And I saw the souls of those who had been beheaded because of the testimony of Jesus and because of the Word of God, and those who had not worshipped the beast or his image, and had not received the mark upon their forehead and upon their hand; and they came to life and reigned with Christ for a thousand years (Revelation 20:4).

*If you wish to order **666/1000** by Salem Kirban ... see Order Form at back of this book.

THE MESSAGE OF THE 144,000

**Preaching
From
Jerusalem**

Right after this terrible persecution of the believers . . . God seals the 144,000 Jews to protect them from this horrible fate so that they might be able to witness of their Messiah to the remaining faithful Gentiles who have turned to Christ and to the still non-believing Jews.

What exactly will these 144,000 preach?

They will preach the same Gospel that Paul and Peter preached; that men are in need of a Saviour; that Jesus Christ died for the remission of sins to provide eternal life for all who but believe!

These 144,000 will not be stationed solely in Jerusalem, but will very possibly be in every part of the globe. And apparently they will all be as effective as a Dwight L. Moody for after they are given the Seal of God we are told:

> And after this I looked, and behold,
> a great multitude, which no one could
> count, from every nation and all tribes
> and peoples and tongues, standing
> before the throne and before the
> Lamb, clothed in white robes, and
> palm branches were in their hands . . .
> (Revelation 7:9)

What a harvest of souls—it will be so great that it will be impossible for an on-looker to count them!

17

A DECREE
THAT BRINGS
DEATH!

A
New
Religious
System

In Revelation 13:15 we read that the False prophet decrees ". . . that as many as would not worship the image of the beast (Antichrist) should be killed."

If you will look back at verse 7 of this same chapter you will read:

> And it was given unto him to make war with the saints and to overcome them: and power was given him over all kindreds, and tongues, and nations.

It is then further revealed how the Antichrist will try to overcome the saints.

And this is how it will happen. He sets up this great religious system with himself (Antichrist) as its god. And in Revelation 13:16-17 we are told:

> And he [The False Prophet] causeth all, both small and great, rich and poor, free and bond, to receive a mark in their right hand, or in their foreheads: (16)

> And that no man might buy or sell, save he that had the mark, or the name of the beast, or the number of his name. (17)

Impossible To Buy Or Sell

A Universal Number

Therefore, in that day it will be impossible to buy or sell without this identifying sign either on the back of your hand or on your forehead. When an individual refuses to submit to the authority of the Antichrist and will not allow this mark to be put on his body, he faces the consequences of either starving to death slowly or else being slain by a representative of the then existing government.

We already see the pattern being laid for this. The Social Security number is fast becoming the universal number in buying a car, in being admitted to a hospital, in securing a loan, etc. The privilege of buying gas on a certain day during the oil shortage depended on whether you had an odd or an even license plate number.

Identifying The Mark

The Number Of Man

What this identifying mark will be . . . the Lord has not desired to make clear to us at this time. Nor can we know at this time the identity of Antichrist.

It may be the number **"666"** which is the number of MAN and stops short of the perfect number 7. Thus **"666"** may well represent the humanistic and sinful counterfeit Satanic Trinity falling short of the divine 777, and catering to lost and fallen man. You will recall man was created on the *sixth* day, and in Daniel 3:1-7 we read where Nebuchadnezzar's image to be worshipped was **sixty** cubits in height, **six** cubits wide and **six** instruments of music summoned the worshippers to worship it.

An Alphabet Code?

Or, it may be that Antichrist's name or title may add up to a total equalling **"666"** using the following ancient number code (this code could be applied to any alphabetical language):

A = 1	F = 6	K = 20	P = 70	U = 300
B = 2	G = 7	L = 30	Q = 80	V = 400
C = 3	H = 8	M = 40	R = 90	W = 500
D = 4	I = 9	N = 50	S = 100	X = 600
E = 5	J = 10	O = 60	T = 200	Y = 700
				Z = 800

The author has received letters from many people speculating on who Antichrist might be.

Another Observation

Rev. Richard Thomas of Ohio suggested that the computer may well become the mechanical monster Antichrist may use to exercise control over the population. In studying this, he came up with the following:

If the number 7 represents perfection, and the number 6 represents imperfection, what if . . .

A = 6	F = 36	K = 66	P = 96	U = 126
B = 12	G = 42	L = 72	Q = 102	V = 132
C = 18	H = 48	M = 78	R = 108	W = 138
D = 24	I = 54	N = 84	S = 114	X = 144
E = 30	J = 60	O = 90	T = 120	Y = 150
				Z = 156

The Computer

Using this numbering system we find the following

$$C = 18$$
$$O = 90$$
$$M = 78$$
$$P = 96$$
$$U = 126$$
$$T = 120$$
$$E = 30$$
$$R = \underline{108}$$

COMPUTER = 666

This certainly is an interesting observation and time will tell. The computer should play a major role in controlling the population. We are seeing how our lives are already, in part, controlled by computers.

Those people who do carry this mark will most likely prefer to have it on the back of their right hand so that it can readily be seen in the act of signing checks and buying.

It is conceivable that the daily papers will contain a list of the names of those who have been killed the day before who have refused to have this mark imprinted on their forehead or on their hand. According to Revelation 20:4, the instrument of death would seem to be the guillotine, or some similar beheading agent.

(Top left) Petra is surrounded by the rugged mountains of Edom. The valley is entered by the Siq—a narrow defile in the red sandstone cliffs. At some places this narrow entrance is only 8 feet wide. Photo at right reveals high red sandstone cliffs which rise 200 to 300 feet. *(Bottom left)* Diane Kirban on horseback. Note numerous caves in background. The area is virtually impregnable from any land attack. See Mark 13:14.

Flee To Petra

Mass Exodus

With the reign of terror which demands that everyone wear the identifying mark of the Antichrist, and with plague judgments of the Lord, there will be a mass exodus in which the Jews and others in Jerusalem will try to flee from this destruction into what to them will be unfamiliar and unfriendly territory.

Some Bible scholars believe the area they will flee to is the city of Petra. Others suggest a flight into the wilderness of the nations of the world.

The Beginning Of The Numbering System

The Trend Has Started

A news article, published in *Time*, March 13, 1972, commenting on a critical Senate Finance Committee vote on the issuing of a Social Security number at age 6, reported:

> Such a system would further enable the Government to amass information on citizens and store it in a central computer under a single identification number. To date, no one has suggested using tattoos.

On March 3, 1972 the Senate Finance Committee voted to direct the U.S. Government to issue a Social Security card to every child entering the first grade after January 1, 1974. Its purpose is to make the Social Security number the universal form of identification for everyone in the U.S.

Such a system will enable the Govern-

The Tatoo System

ment to begin to amass information on each individual at a very early age.

We have become acclimated to numbering systems. The first one to make a widespread use of a number was Adolf Hitler during World War 2. During that war he had the Jews tatooed with identification numbers on their forearms after they were placed in concentration camps.

Pick up the phone to make a telephone call. You dial an area code number. Mail a letter. You use a zip code number. Make a purchase in Sears or any large department store and your credit card with a number is punched into a special new computer that relays that number to a clearing house. Within a few split seconds the machine indicates whether your purchase is approved or denied.

THE ULTIMATE ZIP CODE

You Are Coded

Open a checking account . . . and your checks will bear a magnetic code number. Subscribe to a magazine . . . and you receive a computer number on a card which states, *"Do not fold, spindle or mutilate."*

Federal Government computers maintain millions of files covering every individual in the United States . . . and these are instantly available at the flick of a switch.

West Germany has already issued a 12-digit number to everyone in that country—this number will accompany its holder from cradle to grave.

**Cash
Will
Become
Unpopular**

By 1984, most transactions will be made by a card identification system. Cash will become unpopular. It is quite possible that an invisible tattoo number system for identification will be introduced which becomes visible under special lights.

Many, however, are even today growing weary of having a different number issued to them for everything—their checking account, their savings account, their department store card, their travel credit card, their school number, their auto number, their Social Security number. They ask . . . why not just use **one number**, the Social Security number, for everything? This might even provide the ultimate in Zip codes!

WHO WILL BE THE ANTICHRIST?

by Dr. Gary G. Cohen

The one whom we have called the Antichrist will rise up out of the final ten-king confederation of what was once the Roman Empire (Daniel 7:8, 20-25).

By the end of the first century A.D., when John concluded the New Testament with the Book of Revelation, 95-96 A.D., this ten-king confederacy had not yet come into the world. Thus, that one whom Daniel saw as rising out of it was also not yet in the world (Revelation 17:12).

Bible scholars to this day have attempted to match this final ten-king organization with kings and leagues in world history and have to date been unsuccessful. Time alone will tell if the current frenzy to identify the ten with the European Common Market is correct.

From the fact that Daniel 7 shows the *"Little horn,"* Antichrist, rising from small beginnings and not being part of the original ten, we may conclude that he will not be at the outset one of the rulers of this Revived Roman Empire but will suddenly enter the scene and rise, not without struggle, into its first position of power (Daniel 7:8).

When Antichrist rises his program will incorporate radical and blasphemous social and political changes. There will be great persecution of all those who would give their first allegiance to God and His Christ. We call these the Tribulation Saints (Daniel 7:20, 21, 25). His persecution shall last 3½ years (1 time, 2 times, and ½ time; Daniel 7:25 as confirmed by Revelation 13:5, etc.).

This same world leader appears to be the one who confirms a covenant (=signs a treaty) involving the Land of Israel (Daniel 9:27). He will violate this treaty in some blasphemous manner in Jerusalem at the very site of the ancient Holy Temple (possibly rebuilt in some form at this time). See Daniel 9:27; Matthew 24:15; 2 Thessalonians 2:3-4.

This breaking of the Israel treaty will be coupled with the start of a persecution in the Middle East that will in at least certain aspects be the most horrendous persecution man-hunt in the history of Israel (Matthew 24:15, 21)! The two spirit-filled spokesmen of God, Revelation 11's two witnesses, will at this time be killed and their bodies made a public spectacle to the beholding terrified world, probably watching the main events over TV (Revelation 11:7-10).

WHAT WILL BE HIS MARK?

by Dr. Gary G. Cohen

A second world personality will at this time make his demonic presence felt upon the world that remains. This one will be a counterfeit Holy Spirit, just as Antichrist is the counterfeit Christ and Satan the counterfeit god of this planet.

Because Revelation 13:11 sees him coming out of the *"land"* (KJV *"earth"*) some have guessed that he will arise out of Israel. Others suggest him to be the Pope (compare Revelation 17:9, 18). He will perform wondrous signs and call upon the inhabitants of this world to worship Antichrist, which may merely signify to give him their allegiance (Revelation 13:11-15). This new personality, called the "False Prophet" in Revelation 19:20, will now demand that all who are loyal to Antichrist take a mark upon their right hand or forehead to show this allegiance (Revelation 13:16).

Buying or selling during this period will be difficult and illegal to all who refuse this mark (Revelation 13:17). The conditions of war and famine in the endtime scenario may play a large part in the outward excuse to the world for the necessity of this mark (Matthew 24:6-7; Revelation 6:2,6).

It appears that it will be some sort of credit card number and loyalty badge combined into one. Possibly it may be a tatoo invisible to the naked eye but visible upon some type of light-beam scan.

It will, however, in its numerical aspect have some logo type connection with the number **666**, or a code based on these digits, which will be related directly to the name of the Antichrist (Revelation 13:18). Revelation 16:2 favors a tatoo type mark, here infected as a result of one of God's direct and final judgements. Revelation 14:9-10 shows us clearly that the accepting of this Mark shall involve such a blasphemy against God that it becomes the Mark of the unpardonable sin of that Tribulation age. All who accept it will be eternally lost to the Lake of Fire.

The Antichrist, with his False Prophet, meets his doom at the end of the Tribulation Period, 3½ years after committing his public blasphemous abomination act (Daniel 9:27; Revelation 13:5; 2 Thessalonians 2:3-4). This shall occur when he has his armies, gathered from around the world, about to destroy Jerusalem. This destruction shall come at Christ's coming revelation in power and glory at Armageddon in Galilee (Revelation 19:11-21; 16:16; Zechariah 12:9; 14:4).

18

BIRTH
OF THE
SUPERComputer

**So Small
Yet
So
Powerful!**

The February 27, 1981 edition of *Wall Street Journal* reported that

*More than 15 years ago
a scientist at IBM . . .
suggested that
a new discovery in physics
might be the key to developing a*
SUPERCOMPUTER!

If such a computer could be built (and it will be) . . . this **SUPERComputer** will have the capacity of a dozen of the largest Computers now in use! But look at this: its working parts would occupy a space hardly larger than a grapefruit!

According to Reporter Jerry E. Bishop of *Wall Street Journal,* what started with two researchers in 1967 now involves 150 scientists and engineers. It has been estimated that in the last 10 years, IBM has poured over $100 Million into this project!

What they are attempting to do is cram

1000 tiny electronic switches and
circuits onto a *"chip"* about a quarter-
inch square!

This would become the most powerful computer ever built and plans are to introduce it about 1986.

**Enter
The
MASTER
Computer**

And beyond that **SUPERComputer** will only be a forerunner of a 1990 computer that will become the **MASTER Computer** . . . twenty-five times the capability of the **SU-PERComputer** yet smaller in size than a basketball!

It is interesting to note that the largest users of the giant computers are **banks!** And banks will be the biggest customer for the **SUPER** and **MASTER** Computers!

**Controlled
By
6**

While Computers get more sophisticated, there is one thing they cannot change. They cannot improve upon the time that the electrical signals have to travel from switch to switch.

And look at this revelation:

Specifically, the signals travel through the wiring at the rate of 6 inches per billionth of a second.

Thus, we have another indication that 6 is the Mark identification!

This **SUPERComputer** will be 15-25 times faster than IBM's fastest machine today! The **SUPERComputer** will have the capacity of handling

70 Million to 100 Million instructions per **second!**

Today's machines only handle 7-10 Million instructions per second. Eventually in the late 1980's we will have a **MASTER** Computer capable of handling **250 Million instructions per second!**

What does that mean in relation to Antichrist?

Computer equipment can already perform a multitude of tasks within a few seconds. The above ad appeared in the February 2, 1981 issue of Wall Street Journal. Inset is part of descriptive copy in text of ad.

**Five
Seconds
To
Chaos!**

Let's project the frightening possibilities
. . . remembering that by 1990 the total population of the United States will only be
about 248 Million people!

1. It would mean that in ONE SECOND
   Antichrist could identify every person
   in the United States.

2. It would mean that in ONE more SECOND
   he could identify those who are
   Christians.[1]

3. It would mean that in the third SECOND
   he could identify what street you
   live on.

4. It would mean that in the fourth SECOND
   he could identify how many are in
   your family.

5. It would mean that in the fifth SECOND
   he could program **ALL** the Computers
   in your local Supermarkets,
   Department stores and Banks to
   indicate that you are forbidden to
   make any transactions . . . **forbidden
   to buy or sell!**

Thus . . . in just 5 seconds . . . that is even
less than the time it took you to read this
sentence . . . you would be **DOOMED** by
Antichrist! One moment you and your family would be free. And just 5 seconds later
. . . your ability to live in this present world
would be **SHATTERED!**

---

[1]It may surprise you to learn that most Christians are already identified by computer. Large Christian organizations . . . particularly the big television ministries and right-wing political action groups keep their donors and prospective
donors on computer. Anyone who is knowledgeable in government spying
systems can realize that it will become easy for Antichrist to "steal" the computer data records from Christian organizations without them realizing that
name and address data has even been lifted! This, most likely would not occur
until the middle of the Tribulation Period.

WORLDWIDE MONEY CARD

On New Year's Day, 1981, Greece became the European Community's tenth member. These Common Market nations, totaling some 280 million people, have now become the world's number One economic and trading power.

How long will it be before we see a unified Worldwide Money Card used not only by the 10-nation federation but also by the United States? It could occur within the next 10 years!

 This is the symbol for EUROPA (Europe) UNITED. It now appears on automobiles and on bank credit cards throughout Europe.

U.S. Master computer terminals may be at two loca-
Luxemburg tions: the United States and Luxemburg. Luxemburg, at present, is a Common Market nation but in the future it may serve as Master Computer Headquarters. It now houses the EEC (European Economic Community) Computer commonly called *"the Beast!"* The two blocks will identify which Master Computer should register the transaction.

 This single chip microprocessor will have your entire life history on it. It will identify your food purchasing restrictions, whether you are a Christian, your address, those in your family unit, personality traits, your bank withdrawal limitations plus a host of other data. It will contain 10,000 transistors . . . yet be no bigger than the grid shown to the left. This grid, not any larger than a dime, will determine whether you can buy or sell!

a66687 This series of vertical lines in two blocks plus a
000287771b number and letter code will identify your voice print and will be used to activate "clearance access" at the supermarket check-out counter.

Face Scan You will have your photograph taken by a Face Scan camera. This likeness will appear on your Money Card and a Laser Beam will scan your computer photo to verify your identification.

Universal Numbering System

EUROPA UNITED — U.S. — U.K. — Ireland

☐ U.S. **LUXEMBURG** ☐

SALEM KIRBAN

666 110 215 190 006 117

a 6 6 6 8 7   0 0 0 2 8 7 7 7 1 b   FACE SCAN

Denmark Neth. Belgium France W. Ger. Italy Greece

*Here is what your Money Card **may** look like!*

Besides the various identification cross-match systems described on the page to the left, there may be a universal numbering system. One possible number format is pictured above. Note that it is a series of <u>three</u> sixes **(6+6+6).**

Here is what these universal numbers could represent:

666 This may be the International World Code to activate the Master Computer at central headquarters.

110 This may be the National Code to activate the Super Computer at the United States base station.

215 This would be your phone number Area Code.

190 This would be your Zip Code region number.

006 This would be your Zip Code for the town or city in which you live.

117 This would be your <u>individual identifying number</u> which, in effect, is your personal Zip Code number.

The identification number . . . **666** . . . now appears already on Computers shipped to Israel. It also appears on shirt labels from China, shoes from Italy, floor tile made in the U.S. as well as some Government forms. Strangely enough, the prefix **666** is also used by some department stores in their billing invoices to the customer!

Dr. Mary Stewart Relfe, author of <u>When Your Money Fails,</u> offers some interesting applications on how the number **666** is now in wide use around the world.

19

SATAN'S MARK EXPOSED

**Crisis
Conditions
Trigger
The MARK!**

What set of circumstances will trigger the need to identify everyone with a Mark and exclude believers from buying and selling?

It could be the crisis conditions that come about with an energy shortage. With the price of oil escalating and the Arabs controlling most of the oil resources . . . attention will be focused on the Middle East.

Perhaps an important discovery of oil will be announced. The bulk of the world's oil is located in the Middle East. Suppose that it is revealed that the largest oil find in history has been discovered right in Israel in the area of Caesarea and Haifa!

**Oil
In
Israel**

It is interesting to note that right now exploration for oil is going on in both Caesarea and Haifa. Those who are doing the drilling believe it will be the biggest oil field ever discovered.

**Desire
For
Israel's
Oil!**

Caesarea and Haifa is in the area given to Asher . . . one of the Twelve Tribes of Israel. In Deuteronomy 33:24 we read:

> Let Asher be blessed with children;
> let him be acceptable to his brethren,
> **and let him dip his foot in oil!**

Can it be that Moses foretold some 3400 years ago where the major oil discovery would be in the Last Days? Is the stage being set right now for Armageddon? Time will tell!

The scarcity of energy sources coupled with the dying of the Dollar may bring about a dictatorship government in the United States. It will also force the Common Market nations to unite as one government to insure its existence.

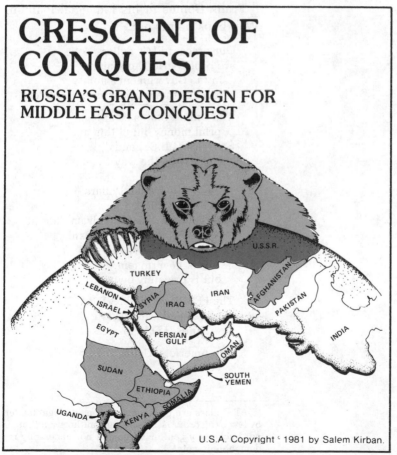

CRESCENT OF CONQUEST

RUSSIA'S GRAND DESIGN FOR MIDDLE EAST CONQUEST

U.S.A. Copyright © 1981 by Salem Kirban.

Russia will seek Israel's oil and Dead Sea minerals.

Road To Dictatorship

Shocking U.S. Debt

Right now the total U.S. debts including long term contracts and loan and credit guarantees comes to almost $10 TRILLION. This is about $125,000 for each and every taxpayer! The interest alone on the national debt is over $120,000 per MINUTE! (That's just the interest, not the principal!)

Frank Goines in his Financial Planning Workbook points out:

Our present FIAT dollars[1]
are based strictly on faith
    in the Government's ability
    to make them appear as legal tender.

The United States can't legally
    print money out of thin air.
So it prints U.S. bonds
    (which, by the way
    are backed up
    by over 8 Trillion Dollars
    of unpaid bills),
and then puts these bonds on deposit
    at the Federal Reserve Bank
    which is not owned by the
        U.S. government,
    but is privately owned.

The FEDERAL RESERVE BANK
    issues Federal Reserve
        Notes (I.O.U.'s) . . .

The American Dollar is extremely
    vulnerable.

---

[1]FIAT Dollars are paper currency made legal tender by law or an order issued by legal authority, although not backed by gold or silver and not necessaily redeemable in coin!

The destruction of the currency
has always brought in a dictatorship.

Lenin, Mussolini, Hitler
and people like this,
were brought into power
through inflation and
the destruction of the currency.[1]

A False Confidence

**Runaway
Inflation**

Inflation is best described as *an increase
in the money supply* or *too many dollars
chasing two few goods.*

Hyperinflation is what occurred in Germany from mid-1922 to November, 1923.
The collapse of the German Mark literally
wiped out the German middle class and was
a major factor in the rise of Hitlerism!

The German monetary system
had no legal gold
reserve requirement
for its notes.

The Federal Reserve System in the U.S.
started out with a 40% reserve.
Today it has no reserve!

Primarily because of the pressure put on
by the money manipulators on Wall Street
for war reparations, the German government resorted to the printing press . . .
printing 250 Billion Marks a week against a
Gold reserve of only 467 Million Marks!

---

[1]Frank Goines, Financial Planning Workbook (Tulsa,
Oklahoma: Prophecy & Economics Newsletter), 1980,
p. 3.

By the end of 1923, the dollar exchange rate was 2.27 U.S. <u>cents</u> for **one billion** German Marks! The Mark depreciated hourly.

German housewives in 1923 found it cheaper to burn worthless marks than to spend them. An inflationary spiral is again threatening many nations. Another such disaster could pave the way for Antichrist!

German workers were being paid as often as three times a day. By October, 1923, 1% of government income came from taxes and 99% from the creation of new money![1]

The Value Of Silver

Rise Of Hyper-Inflation!

<u>Hyperinflation</u> is literally oceans of money that buy less and less until finally the economy collapses and a *"Saviour"* emerges. In Germany, it was Hitler. In the Last Days, it will be ANTICHRIST!

This is why so many people are buying up pre-1964 silver coins by the bagful. Silver retails its buying power . . . paper money does not.

Dr. Mary Stewart Relfe observes:

> In 1969,
> a silver dime would buy a loaf of bread;
>
> In 1979,
> it still would,
>   but it took 80¢ of a paper dollar.
>
> A $10,000 house in 1969
>   could still be purchased
>   for $10,000 in silver coins
>   in 1979
> though its selling price was $100,000
>   in paper money.
>
> The change in worth has not been in
>   silver
> but in the paper dollar.[2]

---

[1]Richard C. Young, A Five-Year Forecast for Gold Prices (Newtown, Connecticut: Silver & Gold Report), February, 1981, p. 5.

[2]Mary Stewart Relfe, Ph.D., Current Events and Bible Prophecy (Montgomery, Alabama: Ministries, Inc.), February, 1981, p. 3.

**$20 Today
Buys
$1 Tomorrow!**

With inflation out of control, the Government solution will be to issue new currency deflating your present currency by 20 to 1. What this means is that 20 of your present dollars will equal 1 new deflated dollar! So while your paper currency will be practically worthless ... any silver, gold or tangible security you have will actually increase in purchasing value!

INFLATION and Deflation

INFLATION
is an increase in the amount of money in circulation, resulting in a relatively sharp and sudden fall in its value and a rise in prices.

Deflation
is a lessening of the amount of money in circulation, resulting in a relatively sharp and sudden rise in its value and a fall in prices.

The Trilateralist's Targets

**Birth
Of
ECU**

Europe, seeing what is happening in the United States, issued new European currency. It is called the **ECU** (European Currency Unit). It was introduced in 1978. The ECU system is gold based. The U.S. dollar is based on the printing press and your faith. Thus we see the dream of the Trilateralists finally coming true . . . the formation of a One World Government! Such a dream will come true at the expense of the United States.

**The
Plan**

The Trilateralists have manipulated two key ingredients to bring the United States to the tragic position it now faces:

1. **Create deficits**
   We are approaching a Trillion Dollar DEBT! We have a mountain of state, city and unfounded private debt. Plus our overseas' debts are monumental.

2. **No Gold**
   Europe has about twice the gold reserves of the United States.

   Plus 80% of the U.S. gold reserve is what is called *"coin melt"* and unsalable on the world market.

What does the future hold for U.S. currency? The United States will be faced with European Common Market currency that is gold based. Thus the U.S. will have to re-issue new American dollars depreciating your present dollar perhaps 20 to 1 or replace the fiat dollar with a gold-backed dollar.

From Collapse To Chaos

**The
Death
Of The
Dollar**

We are already seeing what is happening in corporate failures, real estate failures and cities going bankrupt!

In 1980 Chrysler Corporation reported the worst loss ever reported by an American corporation. They lost $1.7 Billion! And this came despite Congress authorizing a total of $1.5 Billion loan to Chrysler in December, 1979 of paper money!

What caused the Chrysler chaos is the same root problem that brought the rest of America to its knees:

The United States Government printed more paper money to pay its increasing debts . . . which meant issuing more U.S. bonds . . . which meant The Federal Reserve Bank issuing more Notes and increasing the Prime Interest Rate.

With the Prime Interest Rate high . . . business grinds down to a slow pace as purchasing power diminishes.

It's taking more dollars to buy gasoline and many more dollars to buy cars . . . Chrysler (and others) found themselves in chaos!

What you are witness to is the death of the Dollar and the rise of the European Common Market into a position of strength because of its currency base of a gold standard.

The Mark Of Allegiance

Now what does all this mean?

Quite simply it means that Satan is setting the stage for the soon coming Tribulation Period and eventual Armageddon!

It means that the world financial crisis that is upon us will trigger the demand by the people for a leader who will deliver them from the mire of debt and Mideast war crisis.

To achieve this *"heaven on earth"* they will sell their soul! And the price they will pay is allegiance to a world leader.

That allegiance will be demonstrated by wearing his Mark either on your right hand or on your forehead (Revelation 13:16,17).

Whether the Mark of Antichrist is your own personal 9-digit ZIP code or your Social Security number or an 18-number International Money Card only time will tell.

The important thing is not the number or coding system that will produce the Mark. The important thing for all of us to realize is that we **are already** in the Age of the Mark. We are in the Age of ANTICHRIST!

In Our Time?

What God, in His Word told us as long as 2500 years ago is now finally coming to pass! This generation *could* be the generation that witnesses the Rapture of all believers. This generation *could* be the generation that witnesses the emergence of

Is it by chance or design that all cars owned by Arabs in Jerusalem must bear the prefix 666 on their license plate?

On the issuing of a Social Security number at age 6...

"Such a system would further enable the Government to amass information on citizens and store it in a central computer under a single identification number. To date, no one has suggested using tattoos."

TIME, March 13, 1972

ANTICHRIST, the formation of 4-bloc powers that eventually brings on ARMA-GEDDON!

**Time
For
Decision**

Knowing all that we know now as believers ... what great responsibility is on our shoulders to spread the Word to those who know not Christ.

While there is still time turn them from sin to salvation, from following Satan to following the Saviour ... now that you have seen **Satan's Mark EXPOSED!**

20

NO PLACE TO HIDE

**God
Made
A
Way!**

Throughout Scriptures we read of examples of those fleeing from persecution.

About 1530 B.C. Pharoah commanded that every son born of a Hebrew woman be cast into the river (Exodus 1:22).

Jochebed, mother of <u>Moses</u>, hid him 3 months and when she could no longer hide him, she placed him in a little boat made of papyrus reeds. God, in His providence, directed the boat towards Pharaoh's daughter, who had compassion on this little baby whose eyes were filled with tears. <u>Yes, God, made a way!</u>

Under His Wings!

Saul, in a jealous rage, urged his aides and his son Jonathan to assassinate David (1 Samuel 19:1). Jonathan warned David to find a hiding place. In this hide-and-seek chase, David was twice driven into Philistine territory. When aid was given to him by the priests of Nob, Saul had the priests slaughtered and he destroyed the city (1 Samuel 22:17-19). Yet, David, although he had opportunity to kill Saul on two occasions, spared his life. Saul died in battle at Mt. Gilboa. Yes, God, made a way!

From Wealth To Poverty

Job, a wealthy man, with seven sons and three daughters, was the richest cattleman in the entire area of Uz. God allowed Satan to test him (Job 1:12,13). Job lost his children and all his cattle. Then Satan attacked his body (Job 2:4-6) and he broke out in boils and sat among the ashes. And Job's wife told him to:

... Curse God and die.

(Job 2:9)

Job, not helped by his three so-called comforters pleads to God:

*Oh that thou wouldest hide me
  in the grave,
that thou wouldest keep me secret,
  until thy wrath be past ...*

(Job 14:13)

And God answered Job's prayers in His time and gave him twice as much as before (Job 42:10) and Job lived 140 years after that experience of hiding. Yes, God made a way!

Your Life Is Not Your Own

It is difficult for Christians living in North America to understand the terror that comes from persecution, especially when there is no place to hide.

If you find yourself in a position where you are hunted . . . suddenly you discover the democratic system of fair play breaks down.

The Terror Of Being Hunted

**Even
In The
United States**

Only a few in high positions today really know the subtle, illegal methods now being used in government circles to achieve their sinister end. News reports have only touched briefly on this area. It is not something that is peculiar only to the United States. It is practiced in a much greater degree by godless countries such as Russia and China. Spies and counterspies, highly sophisticated surveillance systems, methods of mind control, brain washing, and other more devious devices are practiced daily in today's world. And to ignore the fact that it is going on . . . even in the United States . . . is to bury your head in the sand!

**Soon
Believers
Will Be
The
Target**

At present, these spy activities are mainly directed against communist aggression. But one day soon, they will be directed against Christians . . . with an intensity never before imagined! And for believers, there will be no place to hide!

FIVE WAYS TO CONTROL YOUR LIFE!

Right now, the technology exists to:

1. Keep you from buying or selling. A laser marking system is already a fact!

2. Immediately determine your status. Within 5 seconds a computer can deliver a print-out revealing everything about you and your family, including whether you are a believer and (eventually) whether you contribute to right wing conservative groups and what church you attend!

3. Prevent your wife from conceiving. Contraceptive subdermal implants are *now* ready for the American market. These 6 implants would be placed under the skin of your wife's forearm in a fan-shaped pattern and would prevent her from conceiving for **six** years. The side effects will be nausea, headaches, irregular bleeding and blood tumors.[1]

4. Prevent you from withdrawing your own money from your bank or savings and loan. Computer technology makes it possible to single out believers and deny them the opportunity to withdraw funds . . . or limit them to a figure such as $25 per week!

5. Monitor your every activity and thought patterns! A computer chip (no larger than the size of your little fingernail) can be implanted under your skin. Such a device can transmit signals back to a Master computer terminal and chart your every activity. Sensing devices in the chip can record body changes that, when translated via computer techniques, can discern whether you have negative or positive thought patterns . . . and whether you have an aggressive or passive nature. And if your nature is aggressive and defiant . . . upon instruction, a Computer can trigger the *"spy implant"* to release a long-term tranquilizing drug that will make you subservient to the State!

While this technology, for the most part, is already here . . . it will not be implemented in full until the Tribulation Period. For the believer, that is one consolation as one can see, with this oppression, there will be no place to hide!

---

[1] *Medical World News*, February 16, 1981, p. 56.

The Subtle Designs Of The Enemy

**False
Security**

How does it feel to be hunted and persecuted? Perhaps the greatest insight we can secure is that reported by the China Inland Mission (now *Overseas Missionary Fellowship*).

In 1948, C.I.M. leaders in Shanghai came to the united decision that the Mission should remain in China under a Communist government. Initially, the Communist soldiers behaved very well, paying cash for everything they bought, frequently giving a helping hand to labourers, and assuring

How this event may occur. These illustrations are from **666 Pictorial** by Salem Kirban. If you wish this book, send $4 to: Salem Kirban, Inc., Kent Road, Huntingdon Valley, Penna. 19006. Price includes postage and handling.

everyone that things would go on just as usual, including freedom of worship.[1]

> *"What have we to be afraid of?"* some of the people asked. *"This regime is much better than the old one!"*

A Sudden Change

By 1951, the situation for missionaries became unbearable. Their very lives were in jeopardy. In January, 1951, Director Arnold Lea advised the 637 missionaries and their families to leave China. No one at that time dreamed that the Red Sea trial of exodus would take over 2½ years before every missionary escaped Red China!

A Plea And A Promise

A Prayer Of Faith

Mrs. Mason, a member of the Shanghai C.I.M. staff, prayed, when the situation became critical:

> Lord . . .
> Bring them all out.
> Everyone.
> Let not a hoof — nor a husband,
> be left behind!

That prayer was to become a rallying point of faith for C.I.M. missionaries. For two years they waited as the last two missionaries (Dr. Rupert Clarke and Arthur Mathews) held by the cold and cruel elements of the Red Regime, deliberately tried to starve them.

---

[1]Phyllis Thompson, China: The Reluctant Exodus, (London, England: Overseas Missionary Fellowship), 1979, pp. 35, 36.

There was some inkling of the persecution they would face. It was in a small prayer meeting one morning that Mrs. Joseph Macaulay prayed for these two missionaries:

> O Lord,
> keep their leaf green
> in times of drought!

Times Of Testing

In those two years, Arthur and Wilda Mathews and their baby girl, Lilah, were to experience times when the green leaf came near to withering to a barren brown.

In order to secure a pass to leave China, it was necessary to advertise your intention. If anyone made charges against you . . . the communists had ways of dragging out the interrogations.

Chinese believers were being imprisoned and executed at regular intervals. In order to demonstrate their loyalty to the Red Regime and save their lives, they had to denounce the very missionaries they loved!

Betrayal From Within!

Weak Christians Became Traitors

Any connection, whatsoever, with the "white imperialists" was met with reprisals. Chinese who were weak Christians soon became traitors within the camp . . . spying and relating to the authorities every activity of Arthur and Wilda Mathews.

Black Easter

The pressures seemed unbearable for Wilda. And she remembers March 25, 1951, as Black Easter. It was that day she struck the bottom of despair. It was the final church service with the Chinese as the Red authorities denied Arthur and Wilda the right to attend church any more. The faithful Chinese Christian leader asked everyone in the church to sing, *"He Lives!"*

There Was No Song!

Suddenly Wilda just couldn't sing! If He really *"lives today,"* why had he allowed this? She opened her mouth, but no song came!

Arthur and Wilda rested their case on the Word. And it gave them peace to endure what was ahead. Verses that uplifted them included:

> Ye shall not need to fight
>   in the battle:
> set yourselves,
> stand still,
> and see the salvation of Jehovah
>   with you.
>
> (2 Chronicles 20:17)

> For thou, O God, has proved us:
>   thou hast tried us . . .
> Thou broughtest us into the net . . .
> Thou has caused men to ride over
>   our heads;
>   we went through fire and water:
> but thou broughtest us out
>   into a wealthy place.
>
> (Psalm 66:10-13)

When Only Faith Is Left

Assets Frozen

Up until September, 1951 they were able to withdraw C.I.M. money sent to the local bank in Hwangyuan. The Mathews' mission station was in the great northwest province of Kansu.

Suddenly Arthur and Wilda discovered that Red China had ordered all funds from abroad to be frozen. To add to their testing, there was the terror by night. Communist police would knock at the door late at night ... order everybody out to face the wintry blasts on the pretense of searching the house for spies.

**Down
To
15 Cents**

October 13, 1951 Arthur wrote in his diary:

> Five or six days' coal supply left.
> Fourteen days' flour left.
> Only half a pound of sugar left.

For money, they were down to the small sum of just 15 cents!

The head of the Hwangyuan police force was determined to starve Arthur and Wilda and little Lilah.

Arthur remembers walking up and down in the little icy-cold bedroom singing and praying,

*"Master
the tempest
is raging,*

*the billows are
tossing high ...*

*carest Thou not
that we
perish?"*

The "Belly Crawl"

In order to get any money released from the local bank, Arthur had to make a monthly *"belly crawl."* This experience was devised by the Red Regime to humiliate the missionary.[1]

Each month Arthur had to write out in detail an estimate of the money he would need to buy food and fuel. He would then take this estimate to the sentry at the police station.

Tested And Taunted

More often than not he was told to wait outside in all kinds of weather . . . snow, slush and rain. Waiting all day to no avail . . . he would be told to return the next day. Again he would go through this humiliating experience.

This went on every month . . . waiting for hours, for days . . . only to go home empty-handed. The passersby would taunt him and curse him with foul remarks . . . this to demonstrate to the Red Guard, their allegiance to communism.

The Hardest Trial

The Silent Treatment

The next step of humiliation was even harder to take. Arthur and Wilda lived in a compound of several homes. Three-year-old Lilah enjoyed playing with the Chinese

---

[1] Isobel Kuhn, Green Leaf In Drought Time, (Chicago. Illinois: Moody Press), 1957, p. 75.
Author's note: *I recommend highly that you read this book. It will give you some insight at what persecution is and will challenge you to serve Christ with all your heart!*

children. And Arthur and Wilda still had the opportunity to talk and pray with the Chinese Pastor and friends on the compound. This was to stop. The police ordered that no one was to talk or communicate with the *"white imperialists."* To do so would be to risk death.

Punished For Playing

Lilah was too young to understand why she could no longer play with her playmates. Arthur had to spank her several times to stop her from approaching the other children. It was difficult for him to do. But he knew the consequences and did not want to place these children in jeopardy.

To add to their discomfort, the second floor room was cold in the winter, hot and stuffy in the summer. Below their window was a filthy outhouse which attracted rats, flies and dogs.

How could they tell little Lilah that the Chinese children were not allowed to play or speak to her!

Baby Near Death

It wasn't long before little Lilah came down with dysentery . . . a disease that can kill babies. They had no medicine nor could they get any, despite their pleas. Letters sent for help were mysteriously *"held up."* All that was left for them was prayer. And God, miraculously provided the answer for Lilah's recovery.

The winter of 1952 was bitter. And Arthur and Wilda's plight became desperate. The monthly "belly crawl" to the police station for money was unproductive. They did not have any money for coal.

The Poorest Of The Poor

The Final Humiliation

Finally in September, Arthur was reduced to doing what the very poorest Chinese must do . . . make coal balls.

Coal balls are coal dust mixed with manure and water to make it stick. Arthur, accompanied by little Lilah went on the hillside and joined the poor Chinese. With a sack, a broom and a penknife, Arthur swept up leaves, picked up manure, gathered sticks and cut iris leaves to mold about 50 pounds of coal balls a day.

It did not provide much heat . . . but sufficient to boil water and do the meager cooking. To conserve fuel, often they would sit in the winter sun, patiently molding coal dust with sheep dung and water. The winter water made big cracks in his hands and at times it seemed as though the green leaf would suffer from the drought of testing.

**Free
At
Last!**

In March, 1953, an exit pass was given to Wilda and Lilah. It wasn't until July of that year that Arthur was finally released.

The exodus was complete. Mrs. Mason's prayer had been answered! *"Not a hoof nor a husband left behind!"*

No Change My Heart Shall Fear!

**The
Faith
Of A
Child**

As Arthur and Wilda looked back on their experience one thing that touched them was the unquestioning faith of their little girl, Lilah.

It was breakfast time. Their only fuel was coal balls. Their only food was a rough millet porridge. There was no milk and no sugar.

That evening all they had for supper was toasted bread. Arthur and Wilda were feeling despondent when suddenly little Lilah broke into a song:

> *In heavenly love abiding,*
> *No change my heart shall fear;*
> *And such is safe confiding,*
> *For nothing changes here.*

> *The storm may roar without me,*
> *My heart may low be laid,*
> *But God is round about me,*
> *And can I be dismayed?*

Arthur and Wilda were amazed. They had no idea Lilah even knew these words! **It was the faith of a little child!**

**Insight
Into
Tomorrow**

These experiences of Arthur and Wilda and Lilah should give us some insight of the persecution that believers will face in the

Tribulation Period. Even now, however, the subtle persecutions are beginning. It is a pattern that will reach its terrifying heights in the last 3½ years of the Tribulation.

As in China . . . at first, there will be the semblance of a false peace. There will be religious tolerance. Then, slowly, those who name the name of Christ will be blamed for all the ills of the world.

With the scarcity of food and supplies, believers in Christ will be given limited rations.

Then, they will be segregated. They will find that their mail is held up, examined, censored. Their financial assets will be frozen. Even though they go to the bank to draw out rightfully what is theirs . . . that privilege will be denied.

Soon The Testing Will Come

The Weak Will Fail

They will find many weak Christians turning against them . . . actually spying on them and reporting them to authorities. Friends, relatives, loved ones will break under the pressure and denounce Christians . . . in order to survive and buy food!

Christians will be reduced to either accepting the Mark or facing every type of deprivation and eventually death.

The Final Test

Just as Arthur Mathews was forced to go out on the hillside with the poorest of the poor and make coal balls out of coal dust, manure and water . . . believers will scour garbage cans and rubbish heaps for their very sustenance!

> The mother of Moses
>> sought life for her son.
> And God made a way!

> David,
>> sought a haven from Saul
>> and his army.
> And God made a way!

> Job,
>> sought victory over Satan.
> And God made a way!

Arthur, Wilda and Lilah Mathews, with no place to hide, sought exit visas for a flight to freedom. **And God made a way!**

God Will Make A Way!

One Day Soon!

One day soon, the planned pattern of persecution of Christians will begin. And believers, in desperate trial and agony will cry out to God:

> *Hide me under the shadow of*
>> *Thy wings,*
> *from the wicked that oppress me,*
>> *from my deadly enemies*
>> *who compass me about.*
>
> (Psalm 17:8,9)

And, in confidence, they will know:

> *In the time of trouble*
> *He shall hide me in His pavilion:*

> *In the secret of His tabernacle*
>> *shall He hide me;*
> *He shall set me up upon a rock!*

He is my refuge and my fortress:
My God;
In Him will I trust . . .

Thou shalt not be afraid
for the terror by night;
Nor the arrow
that flieth by day.

(Psalm 27:5; 91:2,5)

God Will Make A Way!

When that time comes when believers feel the sting of Satan, they can sing, as little Lilah sang:

The storm may roar without me,
My heart may low be laid,
But God is round about me,
And can I be dismayed?

That day will come when there will be no place to hide . . . no place . . . but under the shadow of His wings (Psalm 17:8). And when that day comes . . .

GOD WILL MAKE A WAY!

What Manner of Persons Ought Ye To Be!

There shall come in the Last Days
  scoffers,
  walking after their own lusts,
  and saying,
Where is the promise of His coming? ...

But, beloved,
be not ignorant of this one thing,
that one day is with the Lord
  as a thousand years,
and a thousand years
  as one day.

The Lord is not slack concerning His promise ...
  but is longsuffering toward us,
  not willing
  that any should perish,
  but that all
    should come to repentance.

But the day of the Lord
  will come as a thief in the night ...
in which the heavens shall pass away ...
the earth also ...

Seeing then,
that all these things shall be dissolved
  what manner of persons
  ought ye to be
in all holy living and godliness,
Looking for and hasting unto
  the coming
  of the day of God ...

(2 Peter 3:3,4,8,9-12)

Use this ORDER FORM to order additional copies of

SATAN'S MARK EXPOSED

by Salem Kirban

You will want to give SATAN'S MARK EX-
POSED to loved ones and friends.

An excellent book to give to those who
want to know how their world is changing
and want to be prepared for the future,
their future! $4.95

These TWO Books Will Complete Your Series!

**SATAN'S ANGELS
EXPOSED**
Most people are un-
aware that Satan's
subtle deception has
now infiltrated the
Christian church. Spe-
cial section shows
how secret organiza-
tions (like the **Illumi-
nati**) operate to control
the world! Illustrated!
$4.95

**SATAN'S MUSIC
EXPOSED**
Lowell Hart, a former
band leader, is now a
music instructor at
Prairie Bible Institute.
He reveals how con-
temporary music is
making inroads into
the Church and is part
of Satan's plan to water
down its effectiveness.
$4.95

HUMANISM . . . SINISTER, SUBTLE SEDUCTION

Humanism is a deadly philosophy . . . a philosophy that is often used by Satan to deaden the effectiveness of Christian witness. It is a real threat to the Christian School movement. Yet most believers in Christ have no idea how dangerous Humanism really is!

THE TRILATERAL COMMISSION . . . America's New Secret Government

The Trilateral Commission is an extension of the Council on Foreign Relations (CFR). Its ultimate goal is to incorporate Japan, Canada, the United States and the Common Market nations of Europe into a one-world socialistic governmental web.

THE ILLUMINATI

In recent years in Christian circles there have been hushed whispers about the conspiracy of the **ILLUMINATI**. Many believe their aims are to control the world through their arch leader, Satan! This Report traces the history of the **ILLUMINATI** and it may surprise you!

HOW THE MONEY MANIPULATORS KEEP YOU POOR!

We are now living in the Age of ANTI-CHRIST. One real indication of this is that the United States is now controlled in large by powerful foreign interests. "Reveals why the Federal Reserve is neither Federal nor Reserve! The 6-Point Plan to reduce you to POVERTY!

WHAT IN THE WORLD WILL HAPPEN NEXT!

The 1980's will witness chaos, confusion, and a frightening world war! This Report tells you exactly what will happen next! Includes easy-to-understand Charts on Bible prophecy. Makes God's promises in Revelation come alive. Clearly outlines God's 14-point program beginning with the Rapture.

CHARTS ON REVELATION

Salem Kirban has taken the prophetic portions of Scripture and designed clear, concise Charts that any person can understand. You will find this Special Report packed with charts and statistics illustrating every phase of the Tribulation, the Millennium and the New Heavens and New Earth. Excellent to give to loved ones!

THE POWER SEEKERS . . . The Bilderbergers & CFR

The Bilderbergers, the CFR, the Trilateralists all have one thing in common . . . they are secret societies. The Bilderbergers have always been directed by Prince Bernhard of the Netherlands. The Bilderbergers favor an international money system called the "bancor system."

They predicted the recession and many believe both they and the CFR were influential in the control of oil and the rapid price rises of gasoline and heating oils. The CFR seeks an ultimate world order into a united nations. Antichrist will head such a European union!

THE SATANIC TRINITY EXPOSED

One of these days some great leader, admired by the world as a man of peace, will settle the Arab-Israeli dispute. Watch out when this event happens. For the man will become known as the **Antichrist**. His sweet words of peace will soon lead to the most devastating seven years of terror.

Antichrist is a part of the Satanic Trinity *(just as Christ is part of the Heavenly Trinity)*. The counterfeit Trinity is Satan, Antichrist and the False Prophet. A revealing study of their strategy that has already begun!

WHAT IS HELL LIKE?

How sad that many people spend their entire life preparing for a few years of retirement. We are only alloted 60 to 70 years on earth, yet most of our waking hours are concerned with this small unit of time! We never give thought to eternity.

When asked about one's future, many put off making a decision to accept Christ as personal Saviour and Lord of their life. Procrastination is Satan's most effective tool. This Report details exactly what Hell is like. It also clearly explains how to get to Heaven!

USE ORDER FORM ON PAGE 170 ➡

WHAT IS HEAVEN LIKE?

Heaven is a place where believers will receive a new body. There will be no more death, no more tears, no more separation from loved ones in Christ, no more illness, and no night! But there will be so much more! How will your body differ from your present body? Will you recognize your loved ones? These questions and many more are answered fully!

WHAT IS THE TRIBULATION LIKE?

The Tribulation Period will unleash a holocaust of horror such as the world has never seen! It will usher in Antichrist and the False Prophet.

Already we are witnessing the beginning of these sorrows. Events happening right now are preparing us for the Tribulation.

THE SOON COMING BIRTH HATCHERIES

Soon guidelines will be drawn for birth hatcheries to produce genetically *"pure"* babies. Man will seek to improve on God and develop a Master Race. Human babies may be gestated in cows. Sperm banks will become a way of life.

QUESTIONS ASKED ME ON PROPHECY

Where will resurrected Believers live during the Millennium? Will we live again with our mates in Heaven? Are there Scriptures that show that a Believer goes to be with the Lord immediately after death? Do those who have already gone on to be with Christ know what is going on here on earth right now?

SATAN'S MUSIC INVADES THE CHURCH

Many have incorporated the sweet but empty sounds of the world into Christian music in hopes of spreading the good news. But the unholy alliance of pop and rock music with church music is leading many young people into distorted concepts of the Christian life.

THE MARK

Among the facts this shocking report will cover are: The strange Marking System now in your Supermarket ... How the Marking System will be used in Schools ... How you will be controlled by a BEAM of LIGHT ... Why a Marking System must be used by Social Security!

RUSSIA'S RISE TO RUIN!

The saddest fact about Russia's rise in these Last Days is that she will destroy the independent status of the United States and force us to join the Common Market nations as an European conglomerate! Such a move will, of course, usher in the rise of Antichrist.

Now! You can follow Russia's path of conquest through this Special Report. Watch as she topples country after country with her final aim the destruction of Israel and the control of Mid-East oil fields. A revealing study. Includes charts and maps.

I PREDICT

Salem Kirban does not look into any crystal ball. Yet he has an uncanny accuracy for predicting future events! This illustrated Report includes:

- The Year You Change To A New Currency!
- How Satan Will Control Christian Schools!
- The Day A Dictator Rules United States!
- Will 1984 Be The Year Of The Mark?
- Will World War 3 Occur Before 1984?

Also included is *"Why The United States May Not Exist In The Year 2000!"*

THE TRAGEDY OF CHRISTIANS IN POLITICS

A special 32-page Report reveals:

- Why Bob Jones III thinks Moral Majority hastens Antichrist!
- The one key reason why Christians should not get involved in Politics!
- How effective are Christian political action groups?
- How a sleeping giant plans to crush *"religious right-wingers!"*

Plus much, much more including *"Should Christians become a Scriptural Minority?"*

ORDER FORM   KIRBAN REPORTS

Quantity   Description

_____   1/Humanism . . . Sinister, Subtle Seduction
_____   2/The Trilateral Commission . . . America's New
            Secret Government
_____   3/The Power Seekers . . . The Bilderbergers & CFR
_____   4/The Illuminati
_____   5/How The Money Manipulators Keep You Poor
_____   6/The Satanic Trinity Exposed
_____   7/What In The World Will Happen Next?
_____   8/Charts On Revelation
_____   9/What Is Hell Like?
_____   10/What Is Heaven Like?
_____   11/What Is The Tribulation Like?
_____   12/Russia's Rise To Ruin!
_____   13/The Soon Coming Birth Hatcheries
_____   14/Questions Asked Me On Prophecy
_____   15/I Predict
_____   16/The Tragedy Of Christians In Politics
_____   17/Satan's Music Invades The Church
_____   18/THE MARK

TOTAL NUMBER OF REPORTS Ordered [   ]

Reports are $1 each. Minimum Order accepted is $10.
Save by buying in quantity:

1 copy of all 18 Reports $15
                    25 copies $20
                    50 copies $37

You may mix titles to get maximum discount!

☐ **Enclosed is check for $_____ (include $1 for postage).**

☐ **Send 1 copy of all 18 Reports. Enclosed is $15 ($1 for postage).**

(We do NOT invoice. Check must accompany order, please.)

☐ Check enclosed.
☐ Master Charge
☐ VISA

When using Credit Card, show number in space below.

When Using Master Charge
Also Give Interbank
No. (Just above your
name on card)

| Card Ex-pires | Month | Year |

SHIP TO_____
    Mr./Mrs./Miss   (Please PRINT)

Address_____

City_____State_____ZIP_____

SALEM KIRBAN, Inc., Kent Rd., Huntingdon Valley, Pa. 19006

SALEM KIRBAN BOOKS

Salem Kirban is both a news analyst and a recognized authority on Bible prophecy. This unusual combination enables him to foresee trends in economic patterns, in lifestyle, in world power struggles, and in impending disasters! Salem Kirban is the author of over 35 best-selling books! **See Order Form on Page 175.**

CHARTS ON REVELATION
by Salem Kirban $4.95

An excellent teaching aid when studying Bible prophecy. Newly designed crystal clear charts make future events easier to understand. Full color charts on the Rapture, Tribulation Period, Millennium and New Heavens and New Earth! **Includes** God's Promises to Arab and Jew!

COUNTDOWN TO RAPTURE
by Salem Kirban $4.95

How close are we to the midnight hour? Where will it all end? Are we headed for complete chaos? Salem Kirban covers **11** critical areas of change. He also projects a Time Clock showing how close we are in the final Countdown To Rapture. Filled with photos and charts!

GUIDE TO SURVIVAL
by Salem Kirban $4.95

This is Salem Kirban's first book. It sells as well today as when first published in 1968. This new edition has been completely updated and revised. **Almost 300 pages.** This book tells how the world will END. Over 50 photos and Bible prophecy CHARTS!

HOW TO BE SURE
OF CROWNS IN HEAVEN
by Salem Kirban $4.95

Believers must appear before the Judgment Seat of Christ (2 Corinthians 5:10). Here their entire life will be reviewed before God (Romans 14:12). This exciting new book by Salem Kirban shows how you can be **sure** of receiving Crowns in Heaven. Must reading!

HOW TO LIVE ABOVE AND BEYOND YOUR CIRCUMSTANCES
by Salem Kirban $4.95

At last! Here are practical answers to perplexing problems that face Christians everyday. Answers to almost 50 questions that face young people, those who are married and those in the Golden Years of life. Full color! Over 100 photos!

LEBANON . . . A HARVEST OF LOVE
by Layyah A. Barakat
Photo Commentary by Salem Kirban $3.95

This unforgettable true story of how a barefoot girl from Lebanon overcame insurmountable odds to reach her people for Christ. A classic missionary story of trials, testings and final triumph! Full color photographs!

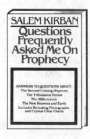

QUESTIONS FREQUENTLY ASKED ME ON PROPHECY
by Salem Kirban $4.95

This new updated version of a popular best-seller will answer those difficult questions many people sidestep. Answers clearly given to questions on Bible prophecy. Includes revealing photographs and crystal clear charts. **Plus added features!**

REVELATION VISUALIZED
by Gary G. Cohen and Salem Kirban $12.75

Enlarged and updated. Excellent for teaching or studying Revelation. Only two verses to a page. Balance of page is explanatory commentary plus charts and photographs. Full Color! **Each verse has Red Arrow pointing to specific Time Period!**

THE RISE OF ANTICHRIST
by Salem Kirban $4.95

While the church sleeps . . . the advance forces of Antichrist have already arrived! Over 20 chapters include: *The Day They Reshape Man, The Plan To Control the Human Mind, The Day They Transplant Memories* . . . plus much more. Filled with PHOTOS!

SEE ORDER FORM ON PAGE 175 →

SATAN'S ANGELS EXPOSED
by Salem Kirban $4.95

At last! Satan's strategy is revealed! Most people are unaware that Satan's subtle deception has now infiltrated the Christian church. Special section shows how secret organizations (like the **Illuminati**) operate to control the world! Illustrated!

SATAN'S MUSIC EXPOSED
by Lowell Hart
Photo Commentary by Salem Kirban $4.95

Lowell Hart was a former band leader. Now as a music instructor at Prairie Bible Institute he reveals how the contemporary sounds making inroads into the Church are part of Satan's plan to water down its effectiveness. Well illustrated!

666/1000
by Salem Kirban $5.95

New! A Double Volume! 480 pages! Two Bestsellers combined into One complete volume! **666** is a novel which vividly captures events as they may occur during the Tribulation. **1000** is a sequel which takes the same cast of characters through the Millennium!

666 (Pictorial Format)
by Salem Kirban $2.95

The entire book, **666,** has been transformed into a **FULL COLOR Pictorial Format.** This 64 page Quality Paperback is excellent for young and old alike. It pictorially describes the Tribulation Period and how the forces of Antichrist operate!

YOUR LAST GOODBYE
by Salem Kirban $4.95

This book tells you all about HEAVEN! It also reveals in clear, easy to understand language exactly what happens **THE MOMENT YOU DIE!** Over 65 charts and photos. Full Color. Over 300 pages! A book with rare information!

SEE ORDER FORM ON PAGE 175 ➜

ORDER FORM

SALEM KIRBAN Books

Quantity	Description	Price	Total
_____	Charts On Revelation	$ 4.95	_____
_____	Countdown To Rapture	4.95	_____
_____	Guide To Survival	4.95	_____
_____	How To Be Sure Of Crowns In Heaven	4.95	_____
_____	How To Live Above Your Circumstances	4.95	_____
_____	Lebanon . . . A Harvest Of Love	3.95	_____
_____	Questions Frequently Asked Me On Prophecy	4.95	_____
_____	Revelation Visualized (September, 1980)	12.75	_____
_____	Satan's Angels Exposed	4.95	_____
_____	Satan's Music Exposed	4.95	_____
_____	666/1000	5.95	_____
_____	666 PICTORIAL FORMAT	2.95	_____
_____	The Rise Of Antichrist	4.95	_____
_____	Your Last Goodbye	4.95	_____
_____	Armstrong's Church Of God (Plain Truth)	4.95	_____
_____	Jehovah's Witnesses	4.95	_____
_____	Mormonism	4.95	_____
_____	Christian Science	4.95	_____
_____	How Juices Restore Health Naturally	4.95	_____
_____	How To Eat Your Way To Vibrant Health	3.95	_____
_____	How To Keep Healthy By Fasting	2.95	_____
_____	The Getting Back To Nature Diet	3.95	_____
_____	The Salem Kirban REFERENCE BIBLE	47.77	_____

Total for Books _____

Shipping & Handling _____

Total Enclosed $ _____

(We do NOT invoice. Check must accompany order, please.)

☐ Check enclosed.
☐ Master Charge
☐ VISA

When using Credit Card, show number in space below.

When Using Master Charge Also Give Interbank No. (Just above your name on card)

Card Expires	Month	Year

POSTAGE & HANDLING Use this easy chart to figure postage, shipping and handling charges. Send correct amount and avoid delay.

TOTAL FOR BOOKS	Up to 5.00	5.01-10.00	10.01-20.00	20.01-35.00	Over 35.00
DELIVERY CHARGE	1.50	2.00	2.50	2.95	NO CHARGE

FOR ADDITIONAL SAVINGS: Orders Over $35.00 Are Now Postage-Free!

SHIP TO_____

Mr./Mrs./Miss   (Please PRINT)

Address_____

City_____State_____ZIP_____

SALEM KIRBAN, Inc./Kent Road, Huntingdon Valley, Pa. 19006

WHAT WILL YOU DO WITH JESUS?

You have just read **SATAN'S MARK EXPOSED!** It may seem too fantastic to be true! But it is! We are living in chaotic times. No event has yet to take place for the *Rapture* to occur. The Rapture is when believing Christians meet Christ in the air.

It should be evident to you that the world is *not* getting better and better. What happens when it comes time for you to depart from this earth? Then, **what will you do with Jesus?**

Here are five basic observations in the Bible of which you should be aware:

1. ALL SIN — *For all have sinned, and come short of the glory of God* (Romans 3:23).

2. ALL LOVED — *For God so loved the world, that He gave His only begotten Son, that whosoever believeth in Him should not perish, but have everlasting life* (John 3:16).

3. ALL RAISED — *Marvel not at this: for the hour is coming, in which all that are in the graves shall hear his voice. And shall come forth; they that have done good, unto the resurrection of life; and they that have done evil, unto the resurrection of damnation* (John 5:28-29).

4. ALL JUDGED — *... we shall all stand before the judgment seat of Christ* (Romans 14:10). *And I saw the dead, small and great, stand before God; and the books were opened ...* (Revelation 20:12).

5. ALL BOW — *... at the name of Jesus every knee should bow ...* (Philippians 2:10).

Right now, in simple faith, you can have the wonderful assurance of eternal life.

Ask yourself, honestly, the question ... WHAT WILL I DO WITH JESUS?

God tells us the following:

... him that cometh to me I will in no wise cast out. (37) Verily, verily (truly) I say unto you, He that believeth on me (Christ) hath everlasting life (47) — (John 6:37, 47).

He also is a righteous God and a God of indignation to those who reject Him ...

... he that believeth not is condemned already, because he hath not believed in the name of the only begotten Son of God — (John 3:18).

And whosoever was not found written in the book of life was cast into the lake of fire — (Revelation 20:15).

Your Most Important Decision In Life

Understanding this, why not bow your head right now and give this simple prayer of faith to the Lord.

My Personal Decision for CHRIST

"Lord Jesus, I know that I'm a sinner and that I cannot save myself by good works. I believe that you died for me and that you shed your blood for my sins. I believe that you rose again from the dead. And now I am receiving you as my personal Saviour, my Lord, my only hope of salvation. I know that I cannot save myself. Lord, be merciful to me, a sinner, and save me according to the promise of Your Word. I want Christ to come into my heart now to be my Saviour, Lord and Master."

Signed . . . .
  Date . . . .

If you have signed the above, having just taken Christ as your personal Saviour and Lord ... I would like to rejoice with you in your new found faith.

Write to me: Salem Kirban, Kent Road, Huntingdon Valley, Pennsylvania 19006, U.S.A. I will send you the booklet **WHAT IN THE WORLD WILL HAPPEN NEXT?** Filled with clear, concise charts and illustrations in full color. It reveals God's 12-point plan from the Rapture to the New Heavens and New Earth. Please enclose $1 to cover packing and mailing costs.